Historical Association Studies

Britain's Decline
Problems and Perspectives

Historical Association Studies
General Editors: Roger Mettam and James Shields

Britain's Decline
Problems and Perspectives

ALAN SKED

Basil Blackwell

First published 1987

Basil Blackwell Ltd
108 Cowley Road, Oxford, OX4 1JF, UK

Basil Blackwell Inc.
432 Park Avenue South, Suite 1503
New York, NY 10016, USA

British Library Cataloguing in Publication Data

Sked, Alan
  Britain's decline : problems and perspectives.
  ——(Historical Association studies)
  1. Great Britain——Economic conditions——19th
  century   2. Great Britain——Economic conditions
  ——20th century
  I. Title   II. Series
  330.941'081   HC255
  ISBN   0–631–15084–6

Library of Congress Cataloging in Publication Data

Sked, Alan, 1947–
  Britain's decline.
  (Historical Association studies)
  Bibliography: p.
  Includes index.
  1. Great Britain——Politics and government——1945–
  2. Great Britain——History——Elizabeth II, 1952–
  I. Title.   II. Series.
  DA589.7.S54   1987   941.085   86–23274
  ISBN   0–631–15084–6   (pbk.)

Typeset in 9.5 on 10 pt Baskerville by Photo-Graphics, Honiton, Devon
Printed in Great Britain by Whitstable Litho Ltd, Whitstable, Kent

Contents

To Vivien, Nicola, Margaret and Nett, who never decline

1 Introduction: Defining Decline

It was only in the 1960s that people in Britain became aware of their 'decline'. Even the Suez fiasco of 1956 had failed to undermine their self-confidence, and in 1959 Harold Macmillan could still win a general election on the slogan 'you've never had it so good.' Yet by the early sixties the mood had changed: de Gaulle's veto of Britain's entry into the Common Market, the political scandals of 1961–3 and the balance of payments crisis of 1964 all forced a public reassessment of the situation. The devaluation of 1967 more than anything else confirmed Britain's 'decline' in the public mind, and since then there has been a flood of articles and books on the so-called 'British disease'. Indeed, for many people, Great Britain has assumed the mantle of nineteenth-century Turkey and become the 'sick man of Europe'. Yet it is still not clear what exactly the sickness *is*, when the disease was first contracted or whether in the long run it will prove to be fatal. The aim of this short book is simply to help clarify these matters.

The easiest, most straightforward and least controversial measurement of Britain's decline is the disappearance of the British Empire. Today, Britain no longer dominates the world; the map is no longer very largely coloured pink; the sun has very definitely set on Britain's imperial past. The Falkland Islands notwithstanding, Britain today is simply a regional power: no longer a world power and certainly not a superpower. Measured by her importance in international affairs, therefore, Britain has incontrovertibly declined.

This aspect of Britain's decline, however, is taken for granted by all and sundry. In the debate over the 'British disease' it is simply not a point of controversy. The disappearance of the *Pax Britannica* is so obvious that it cannot in itself sustain a debate. The *real* controversy is about Britain's 'economic decline' since the Industrial Revolution. Why is she no longer the 'workshop of the world'? Why has she been overtaken by others? The debate, therefore, is really about Britain's '*relative* economic decline' and, logically and ideally, should be the subject of comparative historical research. For in *absolute* terms, of course, there has been no economic decline. Standards of living, indices of production, rates of economic growth – all stand at a record high. People in Britain today are much better

1

off than were their fathers, grandfathers and great-grandfathers. Thus the question at the centre of the debate is really why are they not still better off than the Americans, the Germans or the Japanese? This is the key question to which this book will have to find some answers.

Some commentators, however, have suggested that the 'British disease' is not simply an economic problem. This is not an allusion to the point (considered later) that popular attitudes may influence the economy, but a reference to the fact that, for some observers, Britain has experienced a moral and political decline which can be seen in factors ranging from greater sexual promiscuity, rising crime rates and drug abuse to street rioting, lack of institutional change and the challenge to the traditional party political structure. No one has yet suggested, however, that the moral and political decline of Britain is a more serious problem than her relative economic decline. Hence, we shall examine that topic first.

2 Economic Decline?

By the 1960s progress, especially economic progress, was no longer taken for granted in Britain. The balance of payments crisis of 1964 – leading to the devaluation of 1967 – together with the debate over entry into the Common Market, brought home to the British that however well they had been doing, others had been doing better. Thus, even if the economy since 1945 had grown faster than ever before, it was still performing less well than that of Britain's main economic competitors. The result was a feeling of profound concern and an acceptance of relative decline, which was taking place on a massive scale. By 1980 Britain had been progressively overtaken in terms of gross national product (GNP) per head of population by Norway, Iceland, Finland, Denmark, The Netherlands, Belgium, West Germany, France, Luxemburg, Austria, Australia, New Zealand and Japan, not to mention a number of oil-producing states. In 1985 she was overtaken by Italy. Her present situation, as summed up by one leading economic historian, is as follows: 'Britain is no longer counted amongst the economically advanced nations of the world. A wide gap separates her from the rest of industrialised Europe. The difference as measured in national product per head between Britain and say, Germany, is now as wide as the difference between Britain and the continent of Africa' (Pollard, 1982, p. 3). If this relative decline continues, Britain by the year 2000 will be overtaken in turn by Spain, Greece and Portugal. Yet the outlook could be much gloomier still. As Peter Jenkins wrote in the *Guardian* in September 1978:

> No country has yet made the journey from developed to under-developed. Britain could be the first to embark upon that route. That is what it would mean to move away from a century of relative economic decline into a state of absolute decline. Here is how it could happen.
>
> Productivity continues to increase more slowly than in other countries. Wages grow, at the same rate or faster. Unit labour costs and consumer prices thereby grow much faster. Britain's share of world markets continues to diminish. So does the number of persons employed in manufacture. Export trade ceases to be sufficient to keep factories open while imports strike more deeply into the domestic market. The moment

3

comes at which it is no longer possible to finance a growth in real incomes. Relative decline will have brought about absolute decline.

Today, there are fears that Britain may be approaching that point. Although growth in the economy has revived since 1982, it is still modest and depends to a large extent on North Sea Oil. Manufacturing output is still considerably below what it was in 1979. Moreover, even if the world economy begins to revive, there is the danger that this will only lead to a balance of payments crisis. What then has brought about this situation? Since any examination of the problems involved necessarily becomes a depressing task, perhaps we should begin on a cheerful note by examining a book on Britain's decline that is fundamentally optimistic, the American journalist Bernard Nossiter's *Britain: a Future that Works* (1978).

Nossiter sees the British as fundamentally healthy, decent, vigorous and creative, indeed 'a model for others in the post-industrial age'. According to Nossiter, the British are 'post-industrial' because they have made a 'collective choice' for 'leisure over goods' (Nossiter, 1978, pp. 90, 93). In short, the British would rather work less hard and do without that second car or television set. They are not materialists but sensible, tolerant people with a superior set of values: hence their ability to expel the London smog, to clean up the Thames and entice back salmon, to make London the world capital for the arts and to subsidize art galleries and theatres: 'The money could have been invested to increase productivity in chemicals or ship-building; British society through the budgets adopted by elected governments has chosen otherwise' (Nossiter, 1978, p. 92). Perhaps appropriately, therefore, Nossiter advises Britain to concentrate on tourism which, in 1977, attracted about £3 billion: 'That pays for a lot of imported food and raw materials' (1978, p. 92).

The problem, however, which Nossiter cannot solve, is how Britain is to survive a transition period of de-industrialization before she can be rescued by an economy based on tourism, the arts, micro-chip technology and nuclear power. Besides, his basic analysis is deeply flawed: 'the winter of discontent' of 1979, the urban riots of 1981 and 1985, the recent football hooliganism all cast doubts on the thesis that Britain is particularly civilized or non-materialist. In short, Nossiter can be accused of having mistaken simple inefficiency for a superior set of values. Having rejected the economic arguments for Britain's relative decline, however, he can only ascribe it to the British character which he personally finds attractive. Yet character in the end is not enough, and optimism merely for the sake of optimism cannot be relied upon as a guide to past conduct or future action.

Nossiter's central point – that psychology or sociology rather than economics is at the root of Britain's decline – is not a new one.

Many commentators have pointed to the British dislike of industry, the low prestige of engineers, the bias in favour of the arts, banking, the civil service and law as having something to do with it. Usually, Britain's educational and class systems are mixed up in this type of argument – the classical education of the public schools, training for empire rather than industry, the lack of technical education etc. – all leading to the conclusion that Britain has traditionally lacked entrepreneurial spirit and indeed has been culturally conditioned to despise industry. On most of the questions raised by this sort of argument, however, very little comparative research has been undertaken. For example, it is not immediately evident that a so-called 'class system' was less in evidence in pre-1914 Germany or post-1945 France than it is alleged to have been in Great Britain during these periods. Nor is it immediately apparent that nepotism, the old-boy network, attachment to particular educational institutions or other features of social life have been particularly British phenomena. Nor can it be taken to be an economically irrational act to accept a job in the City or in the professions if alternative careers in industry pay less well or have to be pursued in less attractive surroundings. The choice may well be symptomatic of industry's decline, not contributory to it. Finally, it is difficult to accept, as a recent observer has concluded, that the real reason for Britain's decline is her conversion to 'imperialist values' in the late nineteenth century:

> The argument in this paper, then, is that the nature of British society experienced a fundamental change in the nineteenth century. But the change in question was not simply the familiar transformation from a traditional, rural society into a modern urban and industrial one. Rather the change consisted of the erection in Britain of a type of society, the territorial imperium, with its associated hierarchical and ascriptive status system, which had existed elsewhere in Europe in its basic outlines, but which had hitherto distinguished England by its absence. (Warwick, 1985, p. 126)

This sort of argument is unconvincing on a number of grounds: first, if such a 'fundamental change' really did take place at the end of the nineteenth century, it is difficult to explain why it should have led to only Britain's decline. Both Germany and the USA were also converted to imperialism about this time and at precisely that stage in their economic development when they were overtaking Britain. Japan also became a major imperialist power in the late nineteenth century. Moreover, if imperialist values somehow impede economic growth, it is unclear how France, which was fighting two bitter colonial wars between 1945 and 1962, managed to stage an 'economic miracle' while declining Britain was happily transforming Empire into Commonwealth. Finally, if Britain really did undergo such a transformation, how are her Liberal governments between 1906 and 1914 to be explained? The new imperialism, in sum, simply cannot hold the key to Britain's relative decline; it does not even explain a decline in Britain's own growth rate (which is logically what it ought to do and what Warwick seems to be trying to make it do) since, of course, none took place. Growth in the British economy increased throughout the late nineteenth century, dipped slightly between 1900 and 1907, and then recovered by 1914.

Let us now examine another thesis, that of Martin Wiener (1981), whose *English Culture and the Decline of the Industrial Spirit, 1850–1980* attracted much praise when it first appeared. Wiener argues that the British have simply been conditioned culturally to despise industry, both by their men of letters and by their political and social elites. However, the real trouble with this sort of history is that it is unscientific; in other words, even if it can be shown that many people disliked industry and the industrial process, it cannot be shown how exactly this contributed to Britain's relative decline. Certainly, it is not good enough to argue, as Wiener does, that since most economic historians have failed to explain it in purely economic terms, then we are forced to accept the cultural explanation. This is all the more evident since Wiener's attempts to prove that these cultural factors were specific to Britain fail completely to carry conviction.

Wiener argues that most British writers since 1850 have been opposed to 'the industrial spirit'. Politicians, too, have displayed a preference for the vocabulary and myths of a green and pleasant land. All this stems basically, Wiener argues, from the fact that the bourgeois class of entrepreneurs which made the Industrial Revolution in England was soon gentrified and absorbed into the upper class with its values based on land. There was a different pattern in Germany and the USA because in Germany the bourgeoisie was not similarly absorbed, while in America the industrial spirit was not opposed. The case for this, however, is presented for the American and German models merely by assertion, and for Britain merely by random quotation.

There are a number of further substantial criticisms to be made of Wiener's book. To begin with, it is difficult to accept the argument that only British intellectuals opposed industrialism. For example, one study of American literature discovered that 'in the entire body of modern American fiction ... the businessman [was] almost always depicted as crass, philistine, corrupt, predatory, domineering, reactionary and amoral' (quoted in Hofstadter, 1966, pp. 233–4). Only three business novels presented a positive side to him at all. The USA also suffered from the 'agrarian myth' which, according to Richard Hofstadter, 'was not a popular but a literary idea, a preoccupation of the upper classes, of those who enjoyed a classical education, read pastoral poetry, experimented with breeding stocks and owned plantations or country estates' (Hofstadter, 1955, p. 25).

6

In Germany, too, the intellectuals shunned industrialism. Professor R. Hinton Thomas has written of a cultural tradition in Germany 'with values derived from a society of a different order [which] acquired such aura and authority that when the new industrial reality materialised towards the end of the nineteenth century, this was not easily absorbed into the intellectual context' (Hinton Thomas, 1973, pp. 88–9). Writers such as Lagarde, Heym, Schlaf, Bölsche, Tucholsky and Kraus could, as a result, be quoted in the same way as Wiener quotes their English counterparts.

The real conclusion to be drawn, then, is that industrialization was not particularly welcomed by intellectuals anywhere. This is not, in fact, surprising. Industrialization is not an inherently likeable process and certainly not one which recommends itself to intellectuals who are irrelevant to it. In a wider context, perhaps the last word should be left to Fritz Stern:

> This anti-capitalistic sentiment was of course endemic in the western world; its history has yet to be written and when it is, it most likely will reveal that this anti-capitalistic mood sprang not only from nostalgia for a simple life of some lost Arcadia, but also from nostalgia for a religious faith that seemed doomed to extinction at the same time. (Stern, 1965, p. 91)

A second criticism of Wiener is that he is often naive. It is one thing to quote politicians on the virtue of the countryside; it is another to expect them to say anything else in rural constituencies. Moreover, if politicians retire to farms it is not a mark of their lack of interest in production – old men rarely anywhere retire to factories. Besides, farming in Britain is nowadays very much an industry itself, and often a highly profitable one because of the EEC. Likewise, legislation for 'green belts' is not incompatible with a desire for industrial growth. Konrad Adenauer in Cologne, for example, had constructed one years before the British passed their relevant legislation. Yet no one took this to be a sign of anti-industrialism in the Rhineland. Perhaps Wiener is at his most naive when he assumes that landed values necessarily clashed with industrial ones or that the British landed aristocracy disliked making money. All the most recent research proves him very wrong here.

Nobles and landowners were involved in the process of industrialization everywhere in Europe from the very beginning. Most forge-owners in late eighteenth-century France were nobles. In the German lands, Frederick II of Prussia described the husband of Maria Theresa as 'the greatest factory owner of his age'. Many of the first factories established in nineteenth-century Austria were established by nobles. The idea that the nobility was somehow antagonistic to new sources of wealth is a myth. True, respectability in the nineteenth century demanded the ownership of an estate, and

7

factory-owners everywhere bought into land to acquire respectability if they did not already possess it. But that does not mean that the landowning classes in turn avoided industrial ventures. Far from it. They were often the prime movers in such enterprises. Nor should this have been surprising. In F. M. L. Thompson's words:

> Coal seams and iron ore beds belonged in general to the surface landowners. Transport improvements, canals, harbours, docks and railways required large amounts of land and large amounts of capital. Moreover urban growth, in many ways a phenomenon independent of industrialization, though sharing a common link with population growth, was equally land- and capital-hungry ...
>
> Coal, iron, slate, gravel, clay, houses, even railway lines, these were bountiful crops to grow, and those landowners who adopted a passive rentier stance and allowed others to do the donkey work and risk-taking of their cultivation enjoyed a relatively assured and trouble-free growth in incomes ... As it happened most of them did not adopt a passive, rentier attitude towards the roots of their swelling fortunes, but on the contrary were amongst the foremost risk-takers, and through their agents amongst the most imaginative entrepreneurs, of their times. (Thompson, 1984, pp. 199–200)

One has only to think of the importance of the Duke of Bridgewater to the development of Manchester, the Duke of Devonshire to the development of Barrow-in-Furness and Eastbourne, the Marquesses of Bute to the development of Cardiff and the Duke of Northumberland to the development of Newcastle. Hence Thompson's conclusion:

> The landed aristocracy, if it had ever been un-capitalist or anti-capitalist had certainly gone more than half way towards embracing capitalist methods and ideals by the mid-nineteenth century; hence it is misleading to argue that the drive towards landed status, and the adoption of gentlemanly values, inevitably sapped 'the industrial spirit', turned assertive entrepreneurs who had once been high-achieving devotees of the work ethic and the profit motive into cultured unentrepreneurial gentlemen, and robbed the middle class of its cream by turning it into a simple landed cheese. (Thompson, 1984, pp. 208–9)

In addition, Rubinstein has provided evidence to show that most of the newly wealthy did not invest in land, at least as measured in terms of an estate of 2,000 acres or more. According to his figures, 'considerably less than ten per cent of all Britain's greater landowners in 1883 ... were the products of business and professional wealth created after 1780 (Rubinstein, 1981, p. 137). From Rubinstein's analysis of 45 individual millionaires who did acquire large estates by 1873, it can be shown that only 11 made their fortunes in manufacturing industry (including two brewers), while 21 were in banking or overseas trade, six in minerals and four in railway contracting. Hence, the whole theory of 'gentrification' may be a myth, although Thompson (1984, p. 210) suggests that by the end of the nineteenth century the mere acquisition of a country house might have been sufficient to ensure respectability. His main point remains, however, that even if some part of the business world moved towards the landed class and its values they were met halfway by the latter. And in this process there is no need to assume that the entrepreneurial spirit suffered.

It is difficult, therefore, to accept Martin Wiener's thesis as correct. In the same context, one could go on to discuss a range of theories concerning social relations between the aristocracy and manufacturing bourgeoisie and their implications for the economic fortune of Great Britain. The trouble is that more often than not these theories tell us more about the political views of their proponents than about Britain's economic and social history. Besides, as two leading social historians have written:

Recently, however, the role of the industrial middle class has been subject to much more far-reaching analysis and factual scrutiny. Studies of economic elites in Britain, France, Italy and Austria–Hungary have suggested that, well into the twentieth century, the generators of greatest private wealth were not manufacturing industries but land and finance – the two last often closely interlocked and intermarried. Of the greatest fortunes bequeathed in Britain between 1809 and 1939 only one was made in cotton and one in railways – supposedly the two leading sectors of the Industrial Revolution. Compared with the wealth of the Duke of Westminster (largely derived from urban rents and overseas landownership) or with fortunes amassed in the City of London (notoriously divorced from domestic manufacturing industry) the economic power and personal wealth of individual industrialists begins to look rather slight.

In tandem with the questioning of the *economic* dominance of manufacturers (though largely independent of it) has come a similar questioning of the previously assumed *political* power of the industrial middle class. In the German Empire it has been shown that the participation of businessmen in representative politics rose in the 1880s but declined in the 1900s; executive power remained firmly in the hands of an ennobled civil service and a court-based aristocracy. In Prussia the vast majority of senior local officials and police administrators continued to be drawn from the landed classes. In

France of the third republic, perhaps the most authentically 'middle class' of late nineteenth-century European regimes, bourgeois control of central parliament made surprisingly little impact on the wider and widely ranging structure of French provincial society. In Britain, the nineteenth-century Reform Acts (once celebrated in both Whig and Marxist literature as triumphs of Manchester liberalism) have been reinterpreted as subtle reassertions of aristocratic landowning power. Repeal of the Corn Laws, seen by Marx in *Capital* as Manchester's death-blow to English feudalism, turns out to have been a political coup at least partly supported by and designed to favour the interests of enterprising landowners. Within the actual structure of government, landowners were the most numerous group, in all British cabinets till 1906; and certain key sectors of the civil service (long seen as the heartland of middle-class Benthamite liberalism) remained predominantly aristocratic till 1914. (Harris and Thane, 1984, pp. 215–16)

The same authors conclude 'that class terminology and its application in history should either be confined to ideal types; or preferably, that it should be reworked and developed to take account of a much wider and a more subtle range of historical formations' (Harris and Thane, 1984, p. 229). More relevant to our present purposes, however, is the conclusion that Britain in the nineteenth century does not seem to have suffered economically from a *particularly British* resurgence of landed values or influence. If a more subtle interaction of social relations was taking place in the nineteenth century than most (often Marxist) historians have hitherto assumed, there is little evidence to suggest that Britain in this respect was somehow out of line with developments elsewhere in Europe.

Is there, therefore, no way in which the British experience has differed qualitatively over the past hundred years or so from that of her European and other rivals? If the intellectual and social differences which have hitherto been isolated as causes of decline are disputed, is there any other way in which the problem may be approached apart from the narrow field of economics?

There is, in fact, one approach which may well carry some conviction. The main difference between the history of Great Britain and that of nearly all her rivals or competitors between 1850 and 1960 is surely that of enormous success and continuity: no defeats in war, none in world wars, no civil war, no major colonial wars after 1945, no invasions, no territorial divisions, no collapse of regimes, a high and rising standard of living, world influence on an unequalled scale before 1939 and on a still massive scale even after 1945. The result, perhaps, was a not unnatural pride in British institutions and a willingness to take future success for granted and not to question or reform even the most obvious defects in British society and institutions. Only in wartime or in the immediate aftermath of war would British governments undertake really radical changes or even contemplate them. Very often, too, changes which had already been introduced in wartime would disappear with the return to peacetime conditions. Elsewhere in the world defeat in war, the collapse of regimes and other national traumas resulted in less complacency. Sometimes, indeed ironically, the situation arose where the British introduced changes abroad which they might well have introduced at home: for example, the reform of the trade unions in the British zone of occupied West Germany after 1945, while in Britain itself trade unions were allowed to consolidate their industrially restrictive practices as well as their political influence.

The point to be stressed, therefore, is that Britain's apparent political, economic and international success from 1850 to 1960 almost certainly promoted the attitude that for the foreseeable future British institutions should remain the same. Similarly, it was taken for granted that British markets would remain unchanged, that British society would stay the same and that 'same' would mean 'successful'. Even when by the mid-1960s success no longer seemed secure in economic affairs it was difficult to see what needed changing: attitudes, institutions, policies? This is perhaps even true today. Most people still do not appear to desire much change. Mrs Thatcher's lack of popularity (save when defending traditional national interests and values) attests to this as much as the rise of the Liberal–SDP Alliance. Support for the Alliance, more than anything, seems to represent a desire for a quiet life or in Ralf Dahrendorf's phrase, 'a better yesterday'. Certainly, the Alliance does not appear to represent as radical an alternative set of priorities as Thatcherism or the post-Callaghan Labour party. Hence a century of unmitigated national success, inevitably producing a massive degree of complacency, should be considered one factor in Britain's relative decline.

Let us now, however, turn away from social or attitudinal factors and look at the economic record in purely economic terms. This can best be done by considering the past century in three periods: 1870–1914, 1914–39 and 1939 till the present. In examining these periods, it will be of especial interest to discover whether there were any ways in which Britain proved *peculiarly* deficient economically.

Before beginning, however, it is necessary to examine whether it was in fact merely 'inevitable' that Britain should be overtaken in terms of production by other, larger nations. After all, once they had acquired the technical knowledge to industrialize, once a skilled (and unskilled) labour force became available, would they not have access to greater domestic markets than the British and an equal opportunity in export ones? In fact, did not Britain's 'early start' prove in many ways a handicap later on? Her workforce was more unionized, her equipment less modern, her methods and markets more established and therefore less flexible. Did not all these conditions mean that after a while Britain's lead in world markets was

11

bound to be challenged? The answer, it seems, would have to be yes. Yet this does not in itself dispose of our problem, because critics of the 'inevitability' or 'early start' interpretation have argued that the lead might have been kept longer had Britain responded to the challenge more vigorously. For example, Kirby (1981, p. 6) has written that 'of all the possible responses to foreign competition, British industrialists chose the weakest and most conservative course of action, entering new but markedly less prosperous markets, while remaining heavily reliant upon existing product ranges and techniques of production'. He argues that an early start should have meant more technical experience and know-how, and that therefore the lead should have been kept. Besides, in his view, many of the challengers started with old British-type equipment so that technical change was a problem for them too. Kirby, however, appears to overestimate the time-lags involved in the export of technology in the nineteenth century. For even before the period 1875–1900, during which, in his view, the roots of Britain's economic predicament in the final quarter of the twentieth century are to be found, technology transfers had already taken place which undermined Britain's position. Consider, for example, this statement from Wolfram Fischer:

When the first railways were built in Germany in the late 1830s, no Germany factory was capable of producing adequate rails or equipment. Until 1840 four English firms, two or three Belgian and one American were the sole suppliers of locomotives. The bulk of them came from R. Stephenson in Newcastle, Sharp and Co. in Manchester, Cockerill in Seraing and W. Norris in Philadelphia. By 1853, however, 94 per cent of 729 locomotives in use on the Prussian railways had been built in Germany. More than half of them came from Borsig in Berlin, and other German railways lines were supplied by firms such as Krauss-Maffei in Munich, Kefler in Karlsruhe or Egestorff in Hanover. *It had taken only one decade, from 1842 to 1851, to achieve this dramatic change.* After the middle of the 1850s, Prussian railways (mainly private not state-owned lines) rarely purchased foreign-made locomotives. Those that were imported came from Austria. For all practical purposes German firms were the sole suppliers. In view of the fact that the share of locomotive production within the German machine-building industry rose from under 3 per cent in 1840 to 55 per cent in 1855 and 74 per cent in 1875, it is not surprising that supplying German and other railway networks greatly stimulated the whole field of engineering industries. By quickly adopting British technology, first in textile machinery and later in mechanical engineering Germany had by 1850, become an industrial centre in its own right. (Fischer, 1983, pp. 11–12, my italics)

In other words, as S. B. Saul (1979, p. 11) has put it, 'Germany was able to use British technology and leap forward where Britain had had to find her way and go up many a blind alley – an inevitable disadvantage of an early start.' It seems, therefore, that Kirby possibly underestimates the difficulties involved in holding on to a technological lead. What then of his other assertion that the roots of Britain's relative economic decline today are to be found in the period 1875–1900? It has to be admitted that this is a widespread belief in contemporary Britain.

1870–1914

The case against British industry in the period 1870–1914 is that it eschewed technological innovation; that it relied far too much on 'staples' for exports, that is to say that coal, cotton, iron and steel accounted for more than 70 per cent of exports; that productivity was falling (from 1.87 per cent per annum between 1860 and 1880 to 0.25 per cent per annum between 1890 and 1914); that the British share of world markets was declining as exports grew less rapidly than before and less rapidly than those of the USA and Germany; while, finally, these exports tended to go to a narrow range of export markets located mainly within the British Empire, South America and Asia. As a result, Germany and the USA could overtake Britain by 1914 in terms of industrial production and Germany could take the lead in the 'second' industrial revolution involving chemical products and electrical goods.

Yet there is a counter-case, which states that the British had not lost their entrepreneurial flare, that the British economy was innovating and changing, that its export policies were perfectly 'rational' and that Britain's international financial policies were forming the pivot of an increasingly integrated world economy from which the world as a whole was benefiting. In addition, there is the argument that Germany and the USA were growing more rapidly on account of factors which could not always apply to Britain's more mature economy. Finally, the period 1870–1914 cannot be considered one of uniform decline. Between 1900 and 1914, for example, the economy was probably growing less slowly than at any other time since the late eighteenth century. By 1914 there was an export boom; the rate of growth of manufactured exports revived from 1.6 per cent per annum between 1873 and 1899 to 2.7 per cent between 1899 and 1913; the pound was strong and Britain's current account was heavily in surplus.

Let us now look at the conflicting arguments in more detail, starting with technological innovation, or the lack of it. The argument which concentrates on the 'gentrification' of British industrialists has already been dealt with. The connected argument concerning 'third generation decline', the hypothesis that the grandsons of the founding fathers were no longer interested in business, can

13

also be dismissed. It is simply too hard to find third generation firms before 1914, largely because most had only been established after 1850. In any case those which did exist were not failing. Moreover, the nature of the British economy was changing. As W. Hamish Fraser had written in *The Coming of the Mass Market 1850–1914* (p. 239), 'In most cases British industrialists did succeed in adapting to the constantly changing conditions of the market, of supplies and of resources', while even Kirby (1981, p. 9) admits that 'Britain did manage to maintain an impressive international lead down to 1914 in a number of industries ranging from the armaments sector of heavy industry and shipbuilding to advanced textile machinery and heavy machine tools'. New industries – pharmaceuticals, soap, confectionery – were growing up and the period also witnessed the rise of the multiple chain store and the expansion of international services such as shipping, banking and insurance.

What about the 'staples'? Was there not a lack of technological change there? Did reliance on them not imply a rejection of change in itself? Economic historians, particularly the American 'cliometricians', now appear to doubt this. L. G. Sandberg, for example, in his discussion of the 'entrepreneur and technological change' in this period concludes:

> It is not established that the [technological] failure rate was any higher than in other countries, including the United States and Germany during the same period or than in Britain during earlier periods. Much less has it been shown that the British 'entrepreneurial failures' in this period exceeded those in Germany and America by so much that they can materially have contributed to Britain's relative decline ... Thus to the question: 'Did "entrepreneurial failure" and especially "technological backwardness" play a significant role in Britain's economic decline?' the answer must be 'Probably not'. (Sandberg, 1981, p. 119)

One reason for this is that failures which once seemed apparent no longer do so given the new criterion of 'rationality' developed by cliometricians. Instead of merely assuming that British industrialists could have used techniques introduced elsewhere, these economic historians have put themselves in the place of British industrialists of the time and have discovered that this did not always make sense. For example, it has been shown that any American techniques of cotton spinning would have been uneconomical in Britain – British wages were too high – and that older techniques were better for the rougher yarns used in Britain. In fact, cotton in the years before 1914 was to report record exports. Another example is coal mining. New American techniques were not introduced before 1914. The reasons for this were partly to do with wages: the sliding scale in British mines meant that it was more rational to employ more labour than to use more machinery. Yet geological reasons were also important. To have tried to introduce new machinery into old British shafts would have presented geological difficulties and even risked the collapse of the mines. Finally, here is S. B. Saul on British shipyards:

> The US and German labour forces at that time, unlike the British, included large numbers of recent immigrants to the urban areas coming from Eastern and South Eastern Europe – cheap labour indeed. But not so in Britain where a more stable skilled labour force was the rule, rather than cheap unskilled workers. If so, then the so-called conservatism of British industry, the slowness to move to machine methods, to standardization and to mass production is easily explained and fully justifiable. For those were appropriate methods for the cheap 'unskilled'. This was very true in shipbuilding where British equipment was much inferior to that in German yards but the labour skills were very much higher. Foreign builders lacking this skill had to install expensive machinery to overcome the disadvantages but such investment could only pay if the industry became a mass production one and that neither the Germans nor any other shipbuilding nation could achieve before 1914. Paradoxically, the new equipment laid down abroad if it suited any conditions, only suited the British where there was mass demand, but they did not need it – and so British yards held on to the competitive lead. (Saul, 1979, pp. 23–4)

The old argument about the shortage of technological training and Britain's lack of interest in a scientifically educated economy has also been revised. Sandberg (1981, p. 106) believes that the British avoided sending their foremen, managers and workers to technical schools or colleges because in the British case it was simply more, or at least equally, efficient to train them in the factories themselves through apprenticeship and other schemes. The German historian, Peter Alter (1978) has stressed official British interest in scientific education before 1914 by pointing to the establishment of the National Physical Laboratory (1900), Imperial College (1907) and the Medical Research Committee (1913), as well as to the foundation of new universities at Birmingham (1900), Manchester (1903), Liverpool (1903), Leeds (1904), Sheffield (1905) and Bristol (1909).

It should also be remembered that in making comparisons with German industry it is often not possible to compare like with like. This applies to matters as diverse as statistics (until 1905, it has been estimated that German exports were overestimated by 4 per cent and imports underestimated by 3 per cent), the trade cycle and the make-up of the economies. For example, the differences implied by the existence of cheap mass immigrant labour has already been mentioned. But there were others. One was the boom in urbanization which Germany experienced in the 1880s. Nowhere else in developed Europe did so many large cities grow up so quickly, perhaps nowhere else in the world outside the American Mid-West. S. B. Saul writes that there were 48 German towns in 1910 containing over 100,000 people, that is to say with more than a fifth of the total population, and the rate of growth was high because of the skewed pattern of age distribution:

> The building of endless miles of stucco dwellings for these people formed a perpetual reinforcement of the process of industrialisation that created them – a demand for building materials, glass, water and gas and the vast apparatus of trade and transport that allowed them to function. Not only did it give the electrical industry big investment opportunities in urban electrical works and tramways, but there came the secondary effects in production of steel, copper and lead and at the same time electrical generation needed more coal and the tramways facilitated yet more housebuilding. In Britain in contrast, urbanisation came more slowly – more spread over the century and with established horse and steam transport and gaslighting, electrification of transport and electric lighting were much slower to come about. Railway building too, though it slowed down after the 70s and became much less important to the German economy, still gave it a push that was not present in Britain at the end of the century. (Saul, 1979, pp. 13–14)

This huge boom in urbanization in Germany (and the USA), which was aided by cheap immigrant labour, also meant that these countries could absorb an influx from the land. In Britain, on the other hand, where there was plenty of spare labour anyway and little demand from industry for more at this time, the result was higher unemployment, not faster growth. It should be noted in passing that the German boom was not based on chemicals – a common British assumption. True, Germany had taken the technological lead here, but chemicals only employed 2.3 per cent of the German labour force in this period.

In spite of the German boom, productivity in Germany remained below the British level. In fact, higher British productivity allowed the British to pay higher wages. This was partly because only 7 per cent of Britain's income depended on farming by 1914, whereas the corresponding figure in Germany was 23 per cent. Moreover, British farming productivity was some 30 per cent higher than German. In industry, Britain also held the lead, partly because a much higher proportion of her population was employed in mining (a relatively high-productivity industry) whereas the Germans had 9 per cent of

16

their industrial labour force in pottery, stone and glass and 10 per cent in wood products, all low-productivity industries. The differences between the two countries in metals, engineering and textiles were minimal. But in Germany's high-productivity industry – chemicals – only 2.3 per cent of the work force were employed (as we have already seen). According to S. B. Saul:

> It is important to put the German achievement in perspective: catch up quickly she did but overall her industrial productivity remained below the British. No more than in Britain did the German engineering industry match the specialisation and innovation of the American and a great deal of non-traditional American machinery – typewriters, cash registers, farm machinery – was cheaper and of better quality than the German. Germany was still a relatively undeveloped country in 1914 measured by the share of her population engaged in farming and did not pass average British income levels till the early 1960s. (Saul, 1979, pp. 28–9)

It is time now to look at Britain's role in the international economy in this period. Controversy here surrounds two aspects of British economic behaviour: that her exports tended to go to traditional markets in the Empire, South America and Asia, and that she exported capital on a massive scale. Between 1850 and 1914 about 40 million people emigrated from Europe – to North America, Australia, South Africa and New Zealand. Perhaps not surprisingly, capital followed. The result was that between 1854 and 1914 the cumulative total of British overseas assets grew from £260 million to £4,107 million, mostly in the form of capital investment for railways, harbours and docks. Thus, from 2 per cent of GNP, overseas investment rose to 5.2 per cent of GNP between 1870 and 1913. According to Kirby (1981, p. 14), 'No country before or since has invested as high a proportion of its resources abroad over such a sustained period.' By 1900 indeed the London capital market was being used primarily for foreign investment and more than 80 per cent of its capital issues were designed for overseas investment. By 1914 Britain owned no less than 43 per cent of the world stock of investment overseas, that is to say, in real value, more than all of the overseas investments of the USA today.

It has been argued by some historians that the result of such overseas investment was a capital shortage at home, leading in turn to low investment, low productivity and ultimately to uncompetitive industry, low growth and a loss of Britain's share of world markets. Yet the London money market was the most sophisticated in the world and even regional financial facilities were far superior to those overseas. In the 1880s, too, interest rates were very low. So the true picture which emerges is that there was plenty of available capital, but little demand. In fact, most small firms preferred to re-invest

17

their profits rather than rely on the market. There may even be an irony involved: Saul, for one, argues that 'whereas, for example, in the US industry's response to the inadequacies of the financial structure was to enlarge firm size and to expand on the basis of its own resources, the *adequacy* of Britain's long-term financial institutions put aside the need for such expansion; it was not something forced by marked rigidities. The efficiency of the capital market inhibited fundamental change' (Saul, 1979, p. 17).

It has also been argued that Britain's links to a limited range of export markets in the period 1870–1914 encouraged structural rigidity in the British market. In exchange for cheap primary products from Canada, Australia, New Zealand, South America and Asia, Britain exported her 'staples' and hence lost any incentive to diversify her economy. On the other hand, as we have already seen, the economy did prove capable of diversifying to some extent. British overseas businessmen were in no way irrational in maintaining their export strategies. Investments in staples were after all *secure* investments with moderate to high yields. Traditional trading links also meant cheap food and hence a higher standard of living. Finally, improvements in transport led to favourable terms of trade. It has even been suggested 'that the close economic relations between Britain and her principal suppliers meant that overseas investment was in a sense tantamount to investing in the primary sector of the British economy itself' (Kirby, 1981, p. 16).

Nevertheless, did not these trading links in the long run tie British traders and manufacturers to markets which were one day bound to be lost through protection and to goods which were no longer technologically advanced? Did not the export markets comprise countries which (India excepted) were relatively underpopulated and economically only semi-developed? Perhaps. Yet who is to say what is to happen in the long term? And how long should the long term be? And why should good present-day markets be surrendered or compromised in favour of speculative long-term market changes? How were British exporters of staples in 1870 or 1900 to know about conditions after the First World War or after the Great Crash of 1929? After all, the Germans, who concentrated on European markets, were to suffer from growing European protectionism. Between 1900 and 1914, in fact, world exports of manufactured goods to semi-industrial countries such as India, South Africa, Australia and New Zealand rose by 147 per cent, a considerably faster rate than for similar exports to any other group of countries. And since in 1913 Britain supplied 56 per cent of world exports of manufactures to these semi-industrial countries and Germany only 9 per cent, she 'obviously positively gained in the structure of her trade' (Saul, 1979, p. 22).

The structure of British trade should not be confused with 'imperialism'. This is not the place to enter into a discussion of the defects of the Hobson–Leninist theories of imperialism, yet it should be pointed out that it is by no means clear that Britain benefited from Empire either formally or informally. During this period she was always a free-trading nation with the result that nothing could be imported from her colonies or dominions at a below-world-market price. Imperial preference did not begin until 1897 and even then was so modest as to be of no economic significance. Nor were the consequences of investment in the Empire always directly beneficial. For example, the large sums of money poured into Canada between 1900 and 1914 were mainly used to finance imports from the USA. It must be conceded, on the other hand, that the link with India did help to preserve that particular market for Lancashire cotton. Finally, the costs of Empire were never cheap: men, money, ships, arms and railways all had to be paid for, while other nations were able to trade with the colonies on equal terms and without any of these costs.

Imperialism, like imperial values, therefore becomes something of a red herring in the history of Britain's decline. The real significance of the trading pattern of late nineteenth-century Britain was that it allowed the City of London to become the centre and pivot for an increasingly integrated world economy from which Britain – and indeed all trading nations – benefited. The system worked as follows: Europe, the USA (and later Japan) imported food from the British Empire and ran up deficits. European countries financed their deficits by running surpluses on visible account with Britain and on invisible account with the USA; the latter meanwhile financed its deficits by a visible surplus with Great Britain and Canada. Britain for her part was in deficit on her visible account with the United States, continental Europe and part of her Empire, while running a visible surplus with West Africa, Australia and (particularly) India and enjoying an invisible surplus with everyone. The system as a whole was financed through the City of London and was based on the gold standard, the latter being based in turn on fixed exchange rates, free convertibility and control of domestic money supplies, controlled at first by the movement of gold and later by the movement of interest rates. The gold standard, however, was in practice a sterling one which meant that sterling as a currency was enormously strong.

The whole system could have faced serious problems due to Britain's constant surplus on current account and yet it proved possible to avoid these difficulties partly through Britain's free-trade policies and partly through her overseas investments. Free trade in particular allowed debtor countries to finance their debts by exporting to Britain and thus played a key role in promoting multilateral settlements. It therefore restrained international economic trading rivalries of all sorts. On the other hand, it also involved risks; for example, recessions could spread more easily if world markets were closely interconnected. The growing self-sufficiency of the USA was yet another problem, indeed one which was met only by Britain's massive trading surplus with India. The latter financed no less than two-thirds of Britain's balance of payments deficit and could do so because of special free-trading arrangements with the USA and parts of Europe. Nevertheless, Britain was already facing a potential dollar problem as her deficit with the USA on her visible account increased. The question of the future of the Indian market in this respect would therefore be a critical one.

One school of thought which believed it had the answer to greater economic competition comprised the protectionists who, in the late 1880s under the banner of fair trade and from 1903 behind Joseph Chamberlain's call for tariff reform, proposed to make the Empire a self-contained commercial unit. Yet their programme conflicted with the booming invisible trade of the City (insurance, shipping, banking, investment – worth £340 million per annum by 1914) and the resurgence of the staples in the export markets. Besides, 'Empire trade' was already an anachronism. Since 1880 only one-fifth of British imports came from the Empire (despite its expansion) and India too had vital trading links with the USA and Europe. Thus, in Kirby's words (1981, p. 22), the empire played its part in Britain's well-being only as 'an open dynamic system integrated into the main current of the international economy' and could never have served 'as a defensive mechanism against foreign competition'. Finally, tariff reform might really have over-committed British industry to traditional markets.

How then should the state of the British economy in the period 1870–1914 be summed up? An optimist would say that despite the inevitable catching up by other countries it was still performing well, was beginning to diversify, showed no signs of technological failure, dominated and sustained an international financial system out of which it benefited enormously and adhered to markets which by 1914, however traditional, were in fact booming. True, there were difficulties on the horizon, which included increasing foreign (particularly American) competition, advancing protectionism and, at home, growing labour unrest (a subject which still needs comparative economic research). None the less, the increasing specialization in shipping, banking, insurance, the build-up of huge overseas investments, the rise of new industries (pharmaceuticals, footwear, food-processing, bicycles) and the development of the multiple chain store all gave grounds for optimism. What really went wrong was not business policies or commercial strategy but the outbreak of the First World War which simply destroyed the international economy of which Britain was the centre.

There is almost certainly a great deal of sense in this viewpoint. Yet it can easily be exaggerated. It is very difficult indeed to believe that all apparent technological deficiencies of British industry before 1914 can be explained away by 'rationality'. Even some of the 'cliometricians' are now in revolt against this proposition. Likewise, it is extremely difficult to deny that more diversification was needed or that the interest in scientific education came rather late in the day. On the whole, however, it would still seem to be wise to resist the argument that the roots of Britain's present-day problems are to be found in the period between 1870 and 1914. If peace had continued there is reason to believe that the country could have had time to adjust to new market forces within a favourable international economic environment.

1914–1939

The First World War put an end to the old international economy and to Britain's central place within it. It made the USA the world's leading power economically; it destroyed the export markets for Britain's staples; and it enhanced the economic significance of the new industries in which Britain was under-represented. America emerged from the war with a 20 per cent increase in industrial production and with no need for any economic adjustments. She had provided the wartime needs of her allies and had supplied their old traditional markets. Japan too did very well in the Far East – in India, China and the East Indies. And since Japan had concentrated her economic drive on cotton she threatened Britain's position most. Yet it was not just the rise of the USA and Japan that threatened British markets after the war. Canada and Australia – not to mention China and South America – had become more industrialized with the result that there was much less demand for British staples in these traditional markets too after the war. Worst of all, India had obtained control of her own tariff policies and began to raise her tariffs against British goods, particularly cotton. Demand for coal even fell once petroleum-based transport became more available. The war, moreover, had brought about a glut in shipping and in primary products, causing world prices to fall for commodities produced by countries which traditionally had imported British goods. Britain's trading world had thus fallen apart. Finally, her position regarding invisibles was also no longer so strong. For a start, 10 per cent of her overseas assets had been sold to help pay for the war; secondly, she had a substantial war debt to the United States; thirdly, London's position regarding short-term credit had disappeared; while her lack of a surplus on current account in the 1930s (and lack of a trading surplus throughout the period) meant that she could not rebuild her overseas wealth.

Britain's response was not one of adjustment, however. Rather, there was an overwhelming desire to return to 'normal times'. The re-stocking boom of 1919–20 reinforced this. The result was a return in 1925 to the gold standard with the pound fixed to gold at $4.85. This required a policy of deflation to enforce it, a policy which was applied through 'dear money'. The result, given the international economic environment, was high unemployment. Some historians and economists have argued that a 10 per cent devaluation would have solved a lot of problems. But this view neglects the number of countries which in any case traded in sterling, underestimates the reactions of others and ignores the fact that in many parts of the world in the inter-war period British goods were not wanted at any price. It has also been suggested that Keynesian demand management might have been the answer. Yet a growing consensus of economic historians rejects this. Indeed, an econometric application by Thomas (1981) of Keynes's policies, as outlined in 1929, suggests that they would only have scratched the surface of the problem. Besides, business confidence was absolutely essential for such a policy and neither business nor the Treasury possessed such confidence. Hence deflation prevailed. Even so the 1920s could (despite the million unemployed) register a sort of boom and an albeit much smaller surplus on current account until the Great Crash of 1929. Industrial production between 1920 and 1929 grew by 2.8 per cent and industrial productivity by 3.8 per cent per annum.

Was the economy therefore adjusting after all? Some economic historians have argued that it was, that the technological advances spurred on by the First World War – motor cars, aircraft, advanced machine tools, chemicals, ball-bearings, etc. – had led to more applied science and standardization in new industries such as motor manufacture, electrical engineering, chemicals, paper and printing. Even the staple industries had become more efficient with an 18 per cent rise in productivity recorded in coal mining between 1924 and 1930 and one of 25 per cent in iron and steel production between 1923 and 1930. Other historians, however, ascribe most of this simply to rising unemployment and increased mechanization.

We shall return to the controversy over the significance and productiveness of the 'new industries' shortly. In the meantime, it is important to realize that growth and current account surpluses were still dependent on the international economy which continued to function because, although the USA lacked experience in running the world economy, dollars nevertheless continued to flow abroad, the United States still imported primary produce from abroad and Europe continued to enjoy a balance of payments surplus with these primary producers which enabled her to finance her deficit with the USA. But the weaknesses of the new system – short-term American lending to German banks which in turn lent long; reparations and hot money flows which complicated trade and money cycles; and the refusal of the USA to recognize the link between reparations and war debts – were to overwhelm it after 1929. By 1932 it had collapsed and so Britain had to face an even more severe problem of adjustment than in the previous decade.

Internationally, the 1930s were in all respects difficult for Britain but nowhere more so than in the sphere of international economics. The economy now existed in an autarchic world, yet had been formed in a multilateral trading system. Extreme protectionism, exchange controls and the bilateral balancing of such controls all spelt trouble for Britain's export trade. To these troubles was added the general contraction of export demand that followed the collapse and slow recovery of world output and employment. Yet in the conditions of a world slump, British policies alone could not restore the world economy. Britain therefore had to adjust her position to the new international economic order and did so by a mixture of expedients including leaving the gold standard, imposing tariff restrictions and expanding imperial preferences. There were various other negotiations involved: with the countries of the Empire at Ottawa in 1932; with the South American and Scandinavian states between 1932 and 1934; and with the USA in 1936–8. These last negotiations confirmed the position of the USA as the leading international economic power. But although all these efforts helped exports and the collection of overseas dividends and interest to some degree, 'their overall effect was small' (Drummond, 1981, p. 300). They certainly failed to revive the export trade which, in terms of value or volume, never recovered its 1929 level. By 1938, moreover, Britain's world share of manufactured exports had slightly fallen while her share of exports to the empire had shrunk substantially. In the 1930s, therefore, the British account was unhealthy. From 1931 to 1938 there were deficits every year except for 1935, and the cumulative current account deficit totalled £375 million. Combined with defaults and the decline in value of many overseas assets, this represented an important fall in Britain's net worth. And 'this dreary performance', according to Drummond, was 'especially striking when we recall that Britain herself had become a protectionist country' (Drummond, 1981, p. 301).

Drummond, however, does not believe that it represented 'some sort of fundamental failure' (1981, p. 303), partly because an important part of the problem arose from the overseas property account: 'If overseas property income had flowed into Britain in the 1930s as in the late 1920s, between 1930 and 1938 Britain would have netted an extra £647 million – nearly twice the cumulative deficit on current account during these years' (1981, p. 301). Moreover, although the export record was fairly feeble (77 per cent of the 1929 volume and 67 per cent of the 1913 volume in 1937), 'Britain did not do badly in exporting the products of her newer industries, even under the condition of the 1930s' (1981, pp. 303–4). In 1929 the old staples produced 42 per cent of export receipts and the new industries only 8.2 per cent; by 1937, the corresponding figures were 37 per cent and 21 per cent. Drummond, however, notes that by the same time 'Canadian-assembled motor-cars had already developed a certain market in the UK. Further, by 1939, Japanese and Indian cottons had begun to arrive, while Hong Kong and Singapore were sending some clothes and rubber goods. The "third world" had begun to industrialise; the patterns of the 1960s and 1970s were beginning to emerge' (1981, p. 307).

So much, then, for Britain's attempts to readjust to the changing international economy. Regarding her domestic economy, there are four areas which deserve attention: the emergence of the 'new industries', the 'rationalization' of industrial production as a whole, government policy and industrial relations. The key question is to what extent did any of these improve or retard Britain's industrial performance which overall, particularly between 1934 and 1938, did reasonably well as tables 2.1 and 2.2 demonstrate. In Neil Buxton's words: 'It is when the rate of growth of output per man in this country [Britain] is measured in relation to performance over time that the real achievement becomes apparent. There was a decisive jump in the trend rate of growth from 1.5 per cent per annum between 1870–1913 and only 0.6 per cent per annum between 1900–13, to 2.1 per cent in the period between the wars' (Buxton, 1979, p. 14). He concludes that 'in the 1930s, the growth rate was such in this country as to justify the rise of the term "recovery"', although this description, he agrees, is 'not without its critics'.

What contribution to this 'recovery' was made by the new industries? Richardson (1962) began an important debate by arguing that they were an 'important recovery-inducing force' in the 1930s. Yet this seems improbable. They were still too small a sector of the economy at the beginning of the 1930s to have been able to exert

Table 2.1   Rate of growth of industrial production (per annum)

	1901–13	1913–37	1913–29	1929–37
UK	2.3	2.0	1.3	3.4
Germany	4.7	1.2	0.9	3.0
France	4.2	0.8	2.0	−2.8
USA	4.9	2.9	4.2	0.4
OECD countries	3.9	1.6	1.4	2.2

Source: Buxton, 1979, p. 14.

Table 2.2   Rate of growth of output per man-hour (per annum)

	1870–1913	1913–38	1913–29	1929–38
UK	1.5	2.1	2.1	2.1
Germany	2.1	1.2	0.8	2.1
France	1.8	2.3	2.8	1.6
USA	2.4	3.0	2.8	3.3

Source: Buxton, 1979, p. 14.

such an influence. According to Buxton (1979, p. 18), all of the new industries, with the exception of motor vehicles, were disinvesting by 1932 and 'in the crucial recovery period of 1932–34 accounted for, at the most in any one year, 3.5 per cent of the total net investment undertaken and for 7 per cent of total employment'. At the end of the 1930s the staple industries continued to bulk just as large in the economy. If three of the most important 'new industries' – motor vehicles, electrical engineering, rayon and silk manufacture – in 1937 accounted for 9.7 per cent of the capital stock of manufacturing industry, cotton textiles alone after almost two decades of almost continual decline, still accounted for 8.4 per cent. Finally, if productivity in most new industries rose in the 1930s, so it also did in many of the staples. According to Kirby (1981, p. 74), 'equally impressive achievements were recorded in agriculture, textiles and iron and steel'. It is difficult, therefore, to assign to the new industries more than a contributing role in the recovery of the 1930s, a recovery which in any case had come to an end by 1938 and was thereafter sustained by rearmament policies.

The contribution of 'rationalization' to recovery is also a matter of controversy. Hannah (1974) has shown that in the 1920s an unprecedented number of mergers took place but these, it seems, did not aid growth. According to Kirby (1981, p. 75), 'despite the evidence unearthed by Hannah, concerning the extent of managerial innovation in the interwar period it remains true that there were only two British companies, ICI and Unilever, which developed a relatively advanced multi-divisional structure on the lines of the American General Motors and Du Pont companies as a solution to the managerial problems posed by large-scale organisation.' According to Alford (1981, p. 327), even ICI was hardly a model: between 1927 and 1930 it invested £20 million in a fertilizer plant at Billingham (equivalent to nearly one-third of total fixed capital formation in manufacturing industry in 1930) all of which had to be written off as a gigantic failure. Detailed studies by Coleman (1969) and Alford (1981) show that Courtaulds and Imperial Tobacco also suffered from major deficiencies. Nor did the motor industry or electrical engineering prove highly efficient: mass-produced American radios, batteries and vacuum cleaners flooded the market, while 'in 1939 the six leading British producers, making roughly 350,000 private cars, turned out more than forty different engine types, and even greater numbers of chassis and body models, which was considerably more than the number offered by the three leading producers in the United States making perhaps 3,500,000 cars' (quoted in Alford, 1981, p. 326). Alford's conclusion, therefore, is that no close relationship can be established between changes in scale and productivity:

To whatever degree one stresses merger activity as a force for progress, it has to be recognised that a significant number of mergers were defensive acts in the face of shrinking markets or intensifying competition, and new company names were banners under which loose federations of firms, tied together by financial holding arrangements, operated with a fair measure of individual independence. (Alford, 1981, p. 320)

Hence the general conclusion that seems to emerge is that throughout British industry management remained well behind American levels and was much less willing to adopt modern methods of production than its counterparts in France and Germany. According to a whole range of authorities British management remained resistant to change.

One aspect of the British economy was its poor industrial relations. After the failure of the 1926 General Strike, the unrest of the immediate post-war years died away. Unemployment meant a quieter life for employers, while it was not difficult for them to award reasonable claims to those in work against a background of falling prices. Yet the bitterness of past disputes, especially in the staple industries only hardened attitudes among organized labour. All the old defects, moreover, were soon transferred to the new industries: restrictive labour practices, demarcation disputes, differentials, overmanning. 'It is arguable that the motor vehicle industry again provides the classic example in this respect: it was in the interwar period that the post-1945 pattern of labour relations was established with its multiplicity of unions and all the attendant disadvantages associated with demarcation and wage differentials' (Kirby, 1981, p. 75). In the old industries, meanwhile, despite whatever gains had been or were being made in productivity, Britain still lagged behind her competitors:

For 1936 [Rostas] found that in relation to the corresponding British industries, physical productivity per man in German coalmines and coke ovens was 50 per cent higher, in cotton spinning, rayon and silk between 20 per cent and 25 per cent higher and, in blast furnaces, steel smelting and rolling between 10 and 20 per cent higher. Comparative figures for the USA were even more striking: productivity was substantially higher in all US industries and enormously higher in some, with a maximum difference of 200 per cent for blast furnaces. (Alford, 1981, p. 311)

It was not the new industries or the rationalization of industry, therefore, that was responsible for the upturn in the 1930s. Nor was it the formation of cartels (often legally enforced as in the case of coal) in many industries. The real stimulus came rather from a housing boom encouraged by the government's 'cheap money' policy of the 1930s. British industry for its part had still not adjusted to the challenges of the post First World War world: nor, indeed, according to Correlli Barnett's *Audit of War* (1986), did its record improve during wartime. According to his research, British wartime national production statistics were something of a national disgrace.

1939 to the Present

The impact of the Second World War on the British economy was more profound than that of the First World War. Between 1939 and 1945 Britain sustained an accumulated deficit on current account of some £10,000 million. In order to finance this (not to mention an extra £100 million in foreign and gold reserves), she had received £5,400 million in lendlease and mutual aid from the USA and Canada, sold £1,000 million of some of her most lucrative pre-war foreign investments, requisitioned £100 million of private gold and dollar balances and increased the volume of short-term overseas liabilities (mainly in sterling) by a massive £3,700 million. On the domestic side, there had to be added the costs of internal dis-investment amounting to £3,100 million. Altogether, according to Kirby (1981, p. 82), 'approximate calculations carried out by the Treasury indicated that by the end of 1945 one-quarter of the country's pre-war wealth had been liquidated as a direct consequence of Britain's commitment to the Allied War effort.'

There was a positive side, however. As in 1914–18, the Second World War also aided the process of modernization. The amount of electrical power available to the economy increased by 50 per cent, and at the end of the war the Ministry of Supply had made over $100 million's worth of machine tools (about 20 years' worth) and 75 million square feet of factory space. Moreover, in the words of one writer:

> The iron and steel, machine tool, vehicle, aircraft, chemical, plastic, electrical and electronic industries had all been expanded. The stimulus afforded by war needs to the devel-opment of radar, radio, even simple computers in anti-aircraft defence, provided an invaluable basis for much post war civil development. Chemical substitutes for many raw materials had been known before the war, but the creation of the British petro-chemical industry really dates from 1942 ... Finally, if rail and road transport, the textile and certain other industries had suffered severe disinvestment during the war, the mech-anization of both coal and agriculture had been accelerated. (quoted in Kirby, 1981, p. 102)

The immediate post-war period, however, saw the government confronted with severe economic problems, mainly on account of the 'dollar gap'. With the implementation of the Marshall Plan, however, the getting under way of reconstruction and, later on, the world trade boom which accompanied the Korean War, the dollar gap disappeared and the British economy revived – with full employment. By 1950 Britain had a current account surplus of £297 million and by 1951 exports were 75 per cent greater than their 1938 volume.

British economic history since 1945 can perhaps be divided into three periods: 1945–51, 1951–67 and 1967 to the present. The first comprised the period of post-war reconstruction; the second, the period of growth, of 'Butskellism' and of 'stop–go', a period which ended with the devaluation of 1967, although its end had been in sight, conceivably, since 1962. Since 1967 the British seem to have lived in an era of perpetual economic crisis, fearing that growth will never permanently return and that absolute decline may be just around the corner. That period is still continuing.

There is no space here, unfortunately, to provide a detailed history of these times. The aim of the present discussion is to examine the entire period to try to uncover the roots of Britain's post-war industrial decline. Why was it that virtually everyone after 1945 – the French, the Germans, the Italians, the Japanese, the South Koreans, the Taiwanese, the Singaporeans – enjoyed an 'economic miracle', and Britain did not? In Pollard's words (1982, p. 6): 'the only economic miracle was the British failure to take part in the progress of the rest of the industrial world. Surely it must have required a powerful and sustained effort or most unusual circumstances, to prevent the world boom from spilling over into Britain as well?'

What, then, were the factors peculiar to Britain which explain her dismal record, a record which is typified (a) by regular balance of payments crises every few years since 1947 and (b) by relatively poor economic growth. Smith (1984, p. 81) gives the following figures for European economic growth (percentage increase per annum) for the years 1953–73: France, 5.3; Germany, 5.5; Italy, 5.3; Austria, 5.7; UK, 3.0. This process, it should be remembered, started almost immediately after the war. For, if in the years 1948, 1949 and 1950 output rose at an unprecedented 4 per cent per year and gross domestic fixed investment stood at 15 per cent of GNP, as opposed to the pre-war figure of about 12 per cent, world industrial production by 1948–50 was already growing at 13 per cent, or three times the British rate, while domestic capital formation elsewhere tended to run at well over 20 per cent.

The most recent attempt to explain the post-war trend – and a most devastating one to read – is Sidney Pollard's *The Wasting of the British Economy* (1982). It cannot be denied that this is a powerfully argued work and one which concentrates on features peculiar to Britain's past in an attempt to explain both her relatively poor growth and her balance of payments crises. Pollard sees the key to Britain's relative decline in her poor investment record, which he claims is the result of the sacrifice of the productive economy to the need to maintain the value of sterling. Yet it is an essential part of his case that sterling (which functioned anachronistically until 1972

28

as a reserve currency) was endangered not by any defect in Britain's capacity to trade – the purely private trading account (visibles and invisibles) was invariably in surplus – but by government spending (mainly defence spending) overseas. In short, the British domestic economy was sacrificed to please the international bankers and the military, both of whom showed a contempt for industry and production. This is a case which has been made with more ideological overtones by others, including both Chalmers (1985) and Gamble (1981).

According to Pollard, government spending overseas tipped the current account surpluses into deficit and caused balance of payments crises which were dealt with by deflation. The means involved, however, always included a cutting-back of investment which meant that the economy was unable to respond to the next period of expansion. Bottlenecks would then arise, imports would flood in and soon another balance of payments crisis would begin. Investment would then be cut again, the economy would once more be unable to respond to the swing so that a vicious circle or downward spiral of decline began. And what was declining in particular was the manufacturing base of British industry. This process continued, according to Pollard, from the balance of payments crisis of 1947 right through to 1972 when at last the pound was floated and sterling abandoned its role as a reserve currency. Even this was to make little difference since just at the point when, according to Pollard, it might have been possible to put an end to the decline, a new set of theories was used to cut investment, this time in the name of the money supply. From 1976 onwards the result was yet a new series of cuts in the real economy leading to a new downward spiral: inflationary pressures leading to cuts, leading to unemployment, leading to increased government spending on unemployment relief, leading to an enlarged public-sector borrowing requirement, leading to more cuts, more unemployment and so on, with the productive base of the economy being so reduced that it could not possibly deliver growth. At the same time, Britain was increasing her defence budget and in 1982 even fighting a war over the Falkland Islands. Pollard as a result despairs of any long-term economic recovery.

Some of Pollard's key points had already been made by Manser (1971) in a book entitled *Britain in Balance: the Myth of Failure.* Manser gave the figures for Britain's balance of payments from 1958 to 1969, reproduced in table 2.3, and concluded: 'The plain testimony of the figures, then, is unequivocal. Britain does not run up a commercial deficit. For the cause of her payments imbalance we need look no further than official activity. If there were no Government spending, there would be no deficit, and no balance of payments problem' (Manser, 1971, p. 30). Manser also pointed out the implications of these figures for Germany and Japan:

Table 2.3 Britain's balance of payments figures for 1958–69

	Private balance (£m)	Official balance (£m)	Overall balance (£m)
1958	+558	−410	+148
1959	+367	−479	−112
1960	+76	−533	−457
1961	+605	−541	+64
1962	+625	−611	+14
1963	+584	−619	−35
1964	−78	−666	−744
1965	+425	−677	−252
1966	+706	−754	−48
1967	+332	−793	−461
1968	+387	−785	−398
1969	+1326	−942	+384

Source: Manser, 1971, p. 29. Also reproduced in Pollard, 1982.

Instead of sending their national defence forces overseas, they have been the host of those despatched by others, principally of course the Americans and the British. The German government thus received no less than DM5,347 million on this account in 1968 (about £560 million) and DM4,898 million in 1966 (about £437 million) while the Japanese takings in 1966 were $466 million (about £170 million).

It is instructive to calculate what would have been the balance of payments out-turn for these two countries if, instead of those incoming payments, there had been outflows of the size borne by the UK, i.e. of some £250 million. This clearly would have involved for Germany an absolute turn-around in 1966 of £690 million – from a gain of £437 million to a loss of £250 million. The German balance of payments outcome, overall, for 1966 was a surplus of £92 million. If, then, she had borne the overseas military costs of the United Kingdom, she would have been in overall deficit to the tune of £598 million. The United Kingdom has only incurred a deficit of this size twice since the war, once in 1951 and once in 1964. She had in 1966 a deficit of £128 million. Germany should, therefore, in her enjoyment of balance of payment surpluses be thankful for the exemption from the burden of military costs. The Japanese position is similar. Instead of her actual payments surplus of £120 million, she would have run a deficit of £300 million. There are of course the much-publicised

30

German 'offsets' of her military receipts – the purchases of British goods and loans she has contracted to provide. There is very little firm information on how extensive or effective these offsets are. In any case their intended effect is only to bring the German account back to neutral. They do not add in the actual costs the UK incurs. Even taking the offsets into consideration the Germans would still be in deficit, in the above example, by £160 million. (Manser, 1971, pp. 35–6)

Finally, Manser denied that the British were inefficient or were in any way guilty of 'pricing themselves out of world markets': 'the actual prices charged in world trade', he wrote, 'are unknown; they cannot be, and are not collected by the statistical services' (1971, p. 18). Nor did it matter what Britain sold – the Swiss did well with clocks – while Britain led Europe in research into aerospace, chemicals, electrical goods and computing. All the relevant data, Manser concluded, did not point to 'an inert or inadaptable economy'. In reviewing Manser's book, A. J. P. Taylor wrote: 'It is political dynamite, making nonsense of this country's economic policies over the last 40 years. The pundits greeted it with embarrassed silence' (quoted on the front cover of Manser, 1971).

Others have developed the theories advanced by Pollard and Manser even further. Keith Smith and Malcolm Chalmers, for example, have also stressed the significance of military spending in Britain's decline. In Britain's case, according to Chalmers, 'it has been crucial' (Chalmers, 1985, p. 113). Not only has it led to balance of payments crises, it has also diverted resources from export industries; used up a disproportionate amount of scarce high technology inputs unavailable for civilian application; and taken place at the expense of investment rather than consumption. It is worth considering these arguments in turn.

Concerning the balance of payments crises, Chalmers quotes a 1973 study by Kent W. Rothschild which concluded that 'high military expenditure reduces export availabilities in the machinery and transport equipment sector where chances for export expansion have been above average. This brake on the most expansive sector dampens export growth in general. A slow-down in GNP growth follows from this' (Chalmers, 1985, p. 125). The result is that resources for the modernization of civilian industry have been lost and markets have been taken over by others. Hence, Britain's share of the world market in manufactured exports has fallen from 25.5 per cent in 1950, to 16.5 per cent in 1960, to 10.8 per cent in 1970, to 9.7 per cent in 1980 and only 8 per cent in 1983. Chalmers also enlarges on Manser's analysis of the balance of payments composition, taking the same points for the 1970s and 1980s (see table 2.4). He gives a statistical picture of the relatively high 'military burden' Britain bears (see table 2.5), and from these figures he concludes:

Table 2.4 Britain's balance of payments figures for 1970–81

	Private balance (£m)	Official balance (£m)	Of which military spending (£m)	Overall balance (£m)
1970	+1450	−969	−286	+481
1971	+1945	−940	−299	+1005
1972	+297	−844	−323	−637
1973	−432	−1067	−375	−1499
1974	−1203	−1301	−489	−2504
1975	+93	−1758	−549	−1665
1976	+865	−2087	−664	−1222
1977	+3164	−1443	−753	+1721
1978	+1382	−3426	−731	−2044
1979	−554	−2894	−850	−3448
1980	+2549	−2736	−851	−187
1981	+1703	−3282	−851	−1579
1970–81	+11169	−22747	−7021	−11578
1958–81	+16710	−30330	−9790	−13620

Source: Chalmers, 1985, p. 128.

Even after withdrawal from most European commitments by the early 1970s military spending abroad remained substantial. In 1984–5 estimated net military spending overseas is £1,369 million, which comfortably exceeded the net government contribution to the EEC (£375 million in 1984–5) over which there has been considerably more controversy. As North Sea oil revenues decline and Britain faces renewed balance of payments problems, overseas military spending is likely to become a major political issue – as it did during the 1976–7 sterling crisis. (Chalmers, 1985, p. 129)

The final point made by Chalmers is that Britain's large military budget not only diverts resources from more profitable fields of investment but positively fails to generate much of a 'spin off' for civilian industry. First, it undermines civilian research and development. By 1956, for example, 40 per cent of all professionally qualified scientists and engineers engaged in research and development were working on defence projects. Secondly, almost 60 per cent of these projects were financed from defence funds and nearly two-thirds of the research done by private industry were on defence contracts. The result was that the mechanical engineering industry, shipbuilding and steel employed scarcely any graduate engineers before the 1960s, in marked contrast to the prominent place they

Table 2.5 Percentage of gross domestic product (GDP) spent on defence, 1950–83

	1950	1955	1960	1965	1970	1975	1980	1983
USA	5.1	10.2	9.0	7.6	8.0	5.9	5.6	6.9
UK	6.6	8.2	6.5	5.9	4.8	4.9	5.1	5.6
France	5.5	6.4	6.5	5.2	4.2	3.8	4.0	4.2
West Germany	4.4	4.1	4.0	4.3	3.3	3.6	3.3	3.4
The Netherlands	4.8	5.7	4.1	4.0	3.5	3.4	3.1	3.3
Australia	3.0	3.8	2.7	3.4	3.5	2.8	2.7	2.8[a]
Italy	4.3	3.7	3.3	3.3	2.7	2.5	2.4	2.8
Canada	2.6	6.3	4.2	2.9	2.4	1.9	1.8	2.1
Spain	–	2.2	2.2	1.8	1.6	1.7	1.9	2.1[b]
Japan	–	1.8	1.1	0.9	0.8	1.0	1.0	1.0

[a] 1981 figure.
[b] 1982 figure.
Source: Chalmers, 1985, p. 113.

held in German industry. Ironically, however, Britain still had to look abroad for nuclear weapons and military aircraft, although the proportion of her research and development budget devoted to defence is still extremely high (see table 2.6).

Table 2.6 Percentage of research and development budgets devoted to defence

	1963–5	1966–70	1971–5	1976–9	1980–1 (provisional)
Canada	10.6	7.2	n.a.	3.6	2.7
France	26.2	22.5	18.4	19.6	23.3
West Germany	10.8	10.3	6.9	6.2	n.a.
Italy	2.6	2.4	2.1	1.9	1.4
Japan	0.9	0.9	0.7	0.6	0.6
The Netherlands	1.9	2.3	2.0	1.6	1.5
Spain	2.7	5.1	n.a.	3.3	n.a.
Sweden	34.2	27.3	15.2	14.2	n.a.
UK	34.5	25.6	28.9	29.3	28.0
USA	40.6	31.2	27.7	25.4	23.0

n.a., not available.
Source: Chalmers, 1985, p. 119.

Theoretically, of course, military research could produce benefits for civilian use. Yet in Britain this does not seem to have been the case. For example, such funds were used to subsidize Rolls Royce and to produce that famous 'white elephant', Concorde. Little wonder therefore that N. K. Gardner, according to Chalmers, could report to the Department of Industry in 1976 that since 1945 the total return on £1,500 million (at 1974 prices) invested in the *civil* aerospace industry had amounted to less than £150 million. As the Germans and Japanese recognized, there was little point in competing in this sphere with the USA. This was also true of nuclear power generation where the British failed once again to compete successfully. Yet even in 1981–2 the Department of Energy was spending £172 million out of its research and development budget of £216 million on atomic energy, while only £500,000 was going on energy conservation and less than £1 million on solar energy. The case of naval research is equally depressing. Despite subsidized shipyards and concessionary finance, the message has not yet sunk in that naval and merchant ships must be very differently designed and that 'the community of interest between naval and civil ships research workers can be exaggerated' (Geddes Report, quoted in

34

Chalmers, 1985, p. 121). Finally, not even the arms race offers much of an excuse. True, it brings into Britain £2,400 million a year from abroad. But the return is in fact a poor one. Italy spends only about 40 per cent as much as the UK on defence expenditure, yet has an equal share of the arms market. And France, with a comparable defence budget, earned two and a half times as much during 1979–83. According to Keith Smith, 'the British economic crisis' concerns the fact that if Britain concentrates her research on defence and related projects she will lose all chance of entering modern markets like videos, television computers, digital machines and other consumer durables. Britain will therefore have nothing to sell to offset the balance of payments deficit once North Sea oil runs out. Yet the government ironically sees a crisis of this kind as applying only to the Soviet Union:

It has been estimated that [Soviet] military requirements absorb a third of the output of the important machine-building and useful-working sector. The defence industries thus deprive the civil 'sector of secure resources, particularly skilled management. Unlike the West there is little spin-off from technological advances in the defence sector into the civil economy and this pre-emption of key resources for defence thus inhibits general economic development. (1984 Defence White Paper, quoted in Chalmers, 1985, p. 123)

One set of explanations for Britain's relative decline, therefore, argues that it has been brought about by balance of payments crises often occasioned by government overseas defence spending, crises which in turn have led to the cutting back of investment in the productive side of the economy from which research and development funds and scientists have already been diverted on account of defence policy. These cut-backs in investment have also been necessary, it has been argued, to maintain the value of sterling by retaining the confidence of foreign bankers in the pound.

To what extent can this case be upheld? There is little doubt of the importance which ministers have attached since 1945 to the value of sterling, especially before Britain's entry into the EEC. By 1950 Britain's imports from the USA could already be offset by her surplus with the Sterling Area which was itself in surplus with America. Meanwhile, the sterling balances were about five times as high as the British gold and foreign currency reserves. To risk confidence in these, therefore, meant undermining Britain's currency with ominous and unforeseeable consequences. Governments, however, were not always unwilling to cut their defence and overseas commitments. This happened spectacularly in 1947–8, was meant to happen in 1957, happened in 1967 and again in 1982. However, as one can see, the results were much less radical than were perhaps anticipated. The model therefore seems to fit the facts quite well.

Other economists would none the less cast doubts on many aspects of the thesis.

Cairncross (1981), for example, while admitting that investment in Britain has consistently been lower than in France, Germany, the USA and Japan, attaches little significance to the fact. Where output is faster, he says, so too will be investment: it merely reflects growth, not causes it. In other words, 'investment seems more likely to be symptomatic than causal' (Cairncross, 1981, p. 379). Pollard's reply is to argue that although high investment may not cause growth, low investment will certainly preclude it. Cairncross, however, points out that investment in Britain gives a very poor social yield: 'Britain required twice as much investment [as West Germany] to match a given increase in output' (Cairncross, 1981, p. 380). This suggests that other factors must be taken into account. Cairncross also rejects the argument that Britain has failed industrially to utilize the latest technology: 'research by the National Institute of Economic and Social Research, covering some of the major innovations of the post-war period from float glass to jet engines does not bear this out and suggests that the British record was about average in comparison with other countries' (1981, p. 381). On the balance of payments, Cairncross likewise evinces scepticism. It is 'natural', he writes (p. 384), to infer a connection between 'crises' of this type and sluggish economic growth, but the relationship is difficult to explain. Slow growth might produce low exports. In other words, the balance of payments crises may be the result of slow growth, not vice versa. Certainly, the evidence is that the relative buoyancy of international markets has made little difference to British exports – they could fall when world trade rose and rise when it contracted. Likewise, deflationary policies by British governments have made no obvious difference. It is difficult, therefore, according to Cairncross, not to conclude that this elasticity should be regarded as a 'symptom of the general sluggishness of the economy'. The crises in the balance of payments in any case, he argues, have been overrated. In amplitude and frequency, they were no worse than those suffered by other European countries:

> France for example was in constant balance of payment difficulties in the 1950s and even Japan did not begin to enjoy current account surpluses until well into the 1960s. What does distinguish British trade is the steady decline in Britain's share of world exports of manufactures. This goes back well into the nineteenth century. But the rate of decline has been much faster since the war as the expansion of world trade accelerated while British exports rose comparatively slowly. (Cairncross, 1981, p. 387)

All this gave rise to the notion that there was a need for something called 'export-led growth', despite the fact that there was no logical reason to expect more exports to bring more growth. The opposite, in fact, would be more likely to be true. Cairncross's conclusion, therefore, is: 'If exports can be said to have lagged the lag was not very large and was not obviously decisive. On the contrary it seems much more in keeping with the evidence to regard exports as held back by the same forces and to roughly the same extent as output itself' (1981, p. 388). Here, however, he is not thinking in terms of military expenditure, which he clearly regards as irrelevant to the story. (Others, it should be noted, would agree with him; defence after all is one of government's primary obligations and for a long time after 1945 it was clear for political reasons that it could not be entrusted to Britain's former enemies, the Germans and Japanese. Besides France managed to achieve an 'economic miracle' in terms of growth with a defence budget comparable to ours and despite balance of payments crises. These critics forget, however, that a huge proportion of the French defence budget in the 1950s was underwritten by the USA.) Instead, Cairncross believes that the real constraint on growth in Britain has been bad industrial relations and that the primary blame for these should be assigned to British trade unions.

He is not alone here. Alford, for example, has written that 'anyone with even the slightest interest in Britain's economy since the Second World War can hardly fail to recognise in this a major, if not the single most important, factor in industrial performance – or the lack of it' (Alford, 1981, p. 329). There is certainly plenty of evidence to back this up, much of which is summarized by Gomulka (1978). For example, a study carried out by the University of Birmingham's Department of Engineering Production on the working day of workers in 40 engineering and metal-working firms during the years 1968–72 and a series of case studies of 45 firms in the period 1970–4 showed that on average workers spent 16 per cent of their time 'waiting' to use machines, 48 per cent of their time using them, while for about 50 per cent of working time these machines lay idle. Bacon and Eltis (1976) discovered that machine tools used in British manufacturing were on average no older than in the USA, but that output per machine tool and per man was two to three times greater in the USA. Another study discovered that American firms and multinationals all found British labour considerably less productive than that in France, West Germany, the USA or Canada. Finally, the 'Think Tank' report on the British car industry found that British workers operating the same machines produced only half the output of their West German counterparts. There are many similar studies.

Why should these results apply? Are management or workers to blame? Certainly management cannot be exonerated: there is far too much evidence of bad design, poor quality and bad performance among a wide range of British products. Yet on the issue of productivity most of the blame would appear to lie with the workforce and their trade union representatives. This is not a reference to the old issue of strikes: Professor H. A. Turner of Cambridge demonstrated in 1969 that compared with other countries Britain was not 'strike-prone'. Rather, it is a matter of demarcation disputes and restrictive practices: too many unions inside any given factory, too many men working on one job, too many arguments over who does what, too many machines lying idle at night or during parts of the working day.

> The evidence suggests that when British managements sought to raise productivity by the use of modern methods and equipment they found themselves obliged to accept conditions as to manning, operation or pay that cancelled out much of the advantage of making changes and were not insisted upon by the employees of their competitors abroad. Managements also had to devote much of their time to dealing with labour disputes and to contend with a heavy weight of government regulation that absorbed scarce managerial time and deflected effort from innovating tasks of prior importance to economic growth. (Cairncross, 1981, p. 383)

The reasons behind this situation are well known. Given the rise of unemployment in Britain, which was steady even from a low base after 1945, trade unionists never really believed that full employment was possible. Folk memories of the thirties and before (1926, Tonypandy) also played a part. Innovation was always seen as a threat to jobs, and many shop stewards and union leaders, some of them unrepresentative of their members, had no desire to see the capitalist system work successfully. Management, for its part, with separate canteens, lavatories and other facilities (not to mention different styles of dress and accent) also failed to inculcate in their workforce any sense of identity or firm loyalty. All this resulted in poor industrial relations and productivity.

Both Cairncross and Gomulka (and many others) would add another factor to this picture, namely the lack of what Gomulka refers to as 'growth culture' or what Cairncross describes as 'an environment favourable to business pursuits'. Gomulka (1978) stresses that Western Europe and Japan at various times have been imbued with the need to catch up first with Britain and later with the USA. This has forged a spirit of innovation which success in achieving growth has sustained. Britain, on the other hand, has never felt compelled to catch up, having been a leader in different ways for so long and having become rather 'relaxed' until recently about the achievements of others. Cairncross stresses the alienation of the British elite from industry, mentioning particularly the low prestige of engineers: 'If those who have to plan and carry out economic change in industry enjoy little prestige and include few of the ablest (in point of intelligence) of their generation it is hardly surprising if the rate of change is somewhat slower' (Cairncross, 1981, p. 384).

There is therefore another, quite different, set of theories to explain

Britain's relative decline. The question that immediately arises is whether both sets are incompatible. Together, they represent a kind of chicken and egg problem. Does poor growth cause balance of payments crises and lack of investment or is it the other way round? Are the workers cheated by international capitalism or do they in fact cheat it (and themselves in the process)? Is government policy decisive or does it make little difference? Is the lack of a 'growth culture' the cause or the consequence of poor growth? All these questions must be faced. Probably the answer to the conundrum is that in all cases both explanations are at work at the same time with cause and effect interacting. It is certainly hard to believe that overseas defence expenditure, military research and cut-backs in investment after balance of payments crises have had no effect on growth. Equally, it is difficult to accept that bad industrial relations have not hindered it.

It would seem, therefore, that Britain's relative economic decline can be attributed to a number of factors which taken together seem peculiar to her:

1   the disadvantages of being the 'first industrial nation';
2   a continuous history of success in politics and foreign policy which has encouraged a sense of complacency and discouraged the emergence of a 'growth culture';
3   the outbreak of two world wars which undermined her position at the centre of the world economic system;
4   an unavoidable world role after 1945 which imposed a heavy defence burden on her economy;
5   a system of industrial relations which undermined her productivity.

What then does the future hold? Does low growth matter? If Britain's citizens want better education, better hospitals, better roads and the ability to import foreign goods and travel abroad without being seen as 'third world cousins', the answer would seem to be yes. Peter Jenkins's warning that relative decline can lead to absolute decline and under-development should be taken very seriously. Or, as Pollard puts it, 'The rustic idyll may have its attractions, but it could only be enjoyed by a maximum population of around 10 million. The British population of 55 million cannot exist without urban concentrations and factories, and these have to be efficient. Cairo is not a suitable ideal for London to aim at' (Pollard, 1982, p. 17). Clearly, a great deal will depend on the success or failure of Thatcherism. Will it revive British industry by reforming the unions, changing attitudes towards enterprise and encouraging productivity? Or will it seal Britain's fate by de-industrializing Britain, maintaining her high level of defence expenditure and undermining education and research? It is still too early to tell. We live in very interesting times, however, and should at least attempt to explain them.

3   Moral Decline?

Morality is the code of conduct that regulates the behaviour of individuals towards one another. To some extent it is a matter of private practice, but public morals are enforced by law. This is especially true of matters of sexual conduct where, for example, the state imposes rules concerning the age of consent, contraception and homosexual behaviour. In matters closely related to sexual mores – abortion and divorce, for example – the state also intervenes. Yet there are many people who believe that in all these areas the state either intervenes too little or too much. This is because there is a lack of consensus over the right of the state to interfere in what many regard as areas of strictly private choice. On the other hand, in areas where there is widespread agreement over the state's right to impose rules – to protect the citizen against theft, fraud or bodily harm, for example – the need for criminal law is generally upheld. Finally, there is now a general consensus that good conduct towards others, i.e. morality, should be reflected in public social concern, and that (to take only one example) provision for the poor, the sick and the elderly should be a matter for state action and not simply for private charity.

Hence, in any examination of the possible 'moral decline' of Britain, there are three areas to be examined: first, and by far the most difficult to assess, that type of conduct which is governed partly by private and partly by public morals and which largely relates to sexual issues; secondly, crime in general, about which it ought, in theory at least, to be easier to come to some conclusions; and, finally, social concerns, matters ranging from welfare provision to foreign aid, on which something approaching a consensus has, once again, been manifested. Let us look therefore at these areas in turn and explore whether Britain has experienced a decline in any one of them and also whether her experience has been in any way unique.

Sexual Behaviour

According to Mrs Mary Whitehouse, Britain since the 1960s has been suffering from a 'moral collapse'. This is a view shared not only by Malcolm Muggeridge and Lord Longford but also by powerful figures in political life. Mr Norman Tebbit, for example, as

Chairman of the Conservative Party denounced 'the valueless values of the Permissive Society' in his Disraeli Lecture of 13 November 1985, claiming that 'the trigger of today's outburst of crime and violence' lay in the 'era and attitudes of post-war funk which gave birth to the Permissive Society'. Thanks to 'permissives', he claimed, 'family life was derided as an outdated bourgeois concept. Criminals deserved as much sympathy as their victims ... Violence and soft pornography became accepted in the media. Thus was sown the wind; and we are now reaping the whirlwind.' Indeed, the Conservative party by 1986 was challenging 'permissive values' by emphasizing its own commitment to 'family values', 'Victorian values' or often merely 'the family' itself. Mrs Thatcher told the 1986 Conservative Women's Conference: 'Our policy starts with the family, its freedom and its well-being', while the Education Secretary, Mr Kenneth Baker, legislated to ensure that sex education in schools had to be taught within the moral framework of 'commitment, love and family life'. Meanwhile, the same year saw an attempt by Mrs Victoria Gillick to make it illegal for doctors to prescribe contraceptives to girls under the age of 16 without the consent of their parents. After her defeat in the courts, she too campaigned in favour of Victorian values, exactly the same ones in fact which from the 1960s to the 1980s had been upheld by organizations such as the Festival of Light and Mrs Mary Whitehouse's National Viewers' and Listeners' Association.

Needless to say these attacks on permissiveness gave rise to counter-attacks. Julie Burchill, in an article in *New Society* (13 June 1986), condemned all the fuss about family values and sex education: 'It is wicked of Mrs Thatcher to put forward the family as the answer to a nation's prayer, considering that more than half of all violent assault, more than half of all child abuse, more than half of all murder takes place within the family.' Others simply wondered why Britain was being depicted as particularly permissive. After all, in comparison with other countries, she seemed more reserved than many about the sexual revolution of the 'swinging sixties'. London may have invented the mini-skirt and striptease may have been imported as a cabaret act from Paris, yet live sex shows have never been allowed as happened in France or Scandinavia; homosexual bath-houses have never been established on the model of New York, San Francisco, Paris or Amsterdam; 'singles bars' of the American type have never been introduced; and the incidence of AIDS has been noticeably lower than in the USA, France or Germany. *No Sex Please, We're British* is, after all, still very much a box-office hit in London's West End.

Sex, none the less, is at the very heart of the debate about Britain's 'moral decline'. This may arise, as *Punch* once remarked, from the fact that: 'Whenever sexual morality becomes the motif of public discussion reason flies out of the window' (quoted in Tracey and Morrison, 1979, p. 24). It arises more relevantly, however, because the opponents of 'sexual liberation' or 'permissiveness' regard the implications of 'sexual freedom' as profoundly symbolic. For Malcolm Muggeridge, 'The orgasm has replaced the Cross as the focus of longing' (quoted in Tracey and Morrison, 1979, p. 178). The modern attitude to sex is seen as removing the very need for God. By destroying any sense of guilt or sin which may still attach to premarital, extramarital or 'perverse' sex, the need for redemption and therefore the need for God is also removed. For this reason, sexual intercourse, say the critics of the premissive society, should only be allowed within marriage as a spiritual as well as a physical experience. In Mrs Whitehouse's words: 'The sexual intercourse which a man experiences with a woman is meant to be sacramental – to express the coming together of natural and spiritual powers and experience' (quoted in Tracey and Morrison, 1979, p. 182). Hence premarital sex, but particularly homosexual sex, should never be given moral approval. It is no coincidence, therefore, that Mrs Whitehouse should have instituted a private prosecution against *Gay News* in 1976 for criminal blasphemy for publishing a poem describing the homosexual fantasies of a Roman centurion for the crucified Christ. 'My reaction to it', she said, 'was absolutely fundamental. I think it shook me more than anything I had seen or come into contact with all the time I had been campaigning. I thought it was the recrucifixion of Christ with twentieth century weapons' (quoted in Tracey and Morrison, 1979, p. 3). She was, however, to receive a further blow: 'I was', she added, 'completely overwhelmed by the extent of the opposition, and the silence of the church ... I couldn't believe that there was no member of the hierarchy of the church willing to speak up ...' (quoted in Tracey and Morrison, 1979, pp. 13, 17).

Was such silence a signal proof of moral decadence? After all, a decade earlier, Malcolm Muggeridge had already told Mrs Whitehouse that the stage had been reached when 'the only thing Christians can do is to, as it were, go back to the catacombs; to form as it were a Christian maquis or underground resistance movement. I mean this quite seriously ...' (Tracey and Morrison, 1979, p. 179).

Yet why had the Church not spoken out? Was it tactics, the fear that speaking out might be counterproductive? Or a matter of theology? One bishop after all, has suggested that belief in the divinity of Christ, the virgin birth and the resurrection may all be insupportable. Others, too, have cast doubts on traditional interpretations of the Gospels. Under these circumstances can blasphemy be theologically sustained? Then again, there is the whole issue of homosexuality and its place in Christian thought. At least one prominent bishop and one established theologian have maintained that Christ himself may well have been a homosexual. And a recent prize-winning work of ancient and medieval history disputes the view that the Bible itself condemns the practice. Discussing Christ's position on sexual matters generally, it suggests:

Sexuality appears to have been largely a matter of indifference to Jesus. His comments on sexual mores are extremely few, especially in comparison with the frequency of his observations on such matters as wealth and demonic possession, which were largely ignored by later Christians. Even where sexuality is specifically mentioned, the aim is generally to make a larger point: e.g. using the example of committing adultery 'in one's heart' to point out that it was the intent which constituted sin (Matt. 5: 28). Although he insisted on the indissolubility of the marriage bond, he was widely thought to have advocated celibacy (Matt. 19: 10–12) ... and he certainly rejected the position of paramount importance accorded to the family under Mosaic law and Judaic culture (Matt. 8: 21–22; 10: 35–37; 12: 46–50; 19: 29; Luke 9: 59–60; 14: 26–27; etc.). When confronted with adulterers, he recommended no punishment and clearly suggested that the sins anyone else might have committed were of equal gravity (John 8: 3–11; cf 4: 16–19). He pronounced no condemnations of sexuality among the unmarried and said nothing which bore any relation to homosexuality. The only sexual issue of importance to Jesus appears to have been fidelity: he did not mention the procreation or rearing of children in connection with marriage but only its permanence, and he prohibited divorce except in cases of infidelity. He was apparently celibate himself, and the only persons with whom the Gospels suggest he had any special relationships were men, especially Saint John, who carefully describes himself throughout his gospel as the disciple whom Jesus loved. (Boswell, 1980, pp. 114–15)

The theology of sexual morality, therefore, may not be as simple as Mrs Whitehouse supposes. Yet, it is unlikely that theological scholarship of this kind really underlay the attitude of the Church in 1976. More likely, it saw a need for compassion and had, in any case, already accepted the change from moralist to 'causalist' ethics which characterized all the 'permissive legislation' of the 1960s.

This theme will be elaborated below. Before leaving the sphere of religion, however, it is as well to consider the view that the Church had failed to make a stand lest doing so should have further undermined its apparent decline in popularity. Would a 'reactionary' stand against modern sexual mores have led to more empty pews and smaller congregations? Would the process of secularization have been given a boost?

It should be pointed out that the idea of the Church in decline throughout the twentieth century can be exaggerated. By the 1960s the proportion of the population who were communicants of churches was almost exactly the same as at the end of the eighteenth century, about 15 per cent. True, more people began to attend church during the mid-Victorian era but that was largely due to a rise in the birth rate, the construction of more churches and an influx of Irish and Scots into England. Most Englishmen never attended church except for weddings, funerals and baptisms. In 1851 only one in ten attended church regularly in the big cities and Charles Booth in his surveys of the working class in late Victorian England reported that 'the great masses of the people remain apart from all forms of religious communion.' He wrote: 'the very choir boys when their voices crack promptly claim the privileges of men and give up church going.' Missionaries were needed as a result for 'darkest England' as well as 'darkest Africa' (quoted in Read, 1979, p. 245). The Lambeth Conference of 1897 simply declared that social and economic morality were subjects 'to which numberless Christians have as yet never thought of applying Christian principles' (Norman, 1976, p. 4). Indeed, the reaction against the Church had already set in before the end of Victoria's reign. Thus, in 1886 in the Church of England 814 priests were ordained; but in 1901 only 569. The decline was not, however, consistent. Between 1931 and 1941, for example, there was an increase of 29.8 per cent in the number of priests ordained in the Catholic Church; between 1941 and 1951 an increase of 15.3 per cent; between 1951 and 1961 an increase of 11 per cent; and between 1961 and 1966 an increase of 6.8 per cent. Only after 1966 was an absolute decrease experienced. The Anglican Church meanwhile saw a drop in annual ordination between 1963 and 1973 from 632 to 373. It is therefore difficult to establish a steady decline in Christianity in Britain since the Victorian era. In the 1960s some 90 per cent of the English population still claimed a religious affiliation: 60 per cent Anglican, 12 per cent Roman Catholic, 11 per cent Free Church, 1 per cent Jews, 5 per cent other faiths, 5 per cent no religion. What it all meant, however, is far from clear. One opinion poll (quoted in Tracey and Morrison, 1979, p. 28) found that of those attending Anglican services 40 per cent did not believe in life after death; 26 per cent of doubters, agnostics and atheists prayed; and 20 per cent of this second group said Christ was more than a man.

The most recent research on the subject (Abrams et al., 1985) reveals that, while in Britain over 70 per cent of the population seldom or never read the Bible, while no more than one person in seven attends church weekly and while less than one-fifth of the population comprises convinced Christians, three-quarters express a belief in God, 85 per cent report membership of one of the main Christian denominations, only 2 per cent claim to be convinced atheists and there is widespread support for traditional Christian morality as expressed in the Ten Commandments. This rather confused picture of a partially absorbed but declining Christianity is borne out by table 3.1.

It is little wonder therefore that many commentators have themselves been confused by British religious views. Probably most Victorians felt likewise. The Victorians, however, were worse off in

Table 3.1 Percentage endorsement of traditional religious values by social class and age

Item	Total sample	Social class			Age		
		ABC1	C2	DE	18–34	35–54	55+
Believe in God	76	73	74	81	65	79	85
Suicide unjustified	72	70	74	74	67	71	80
Life never meaningless	50	50	54	46	44	51	58
Killing in self-defence unjustified	46	43	49	48	39	45	56
Comfort from religion	46	46	40	52	28	46	67
Disagree future uncertain	37	40	38	32	31	33	25
Often think about life	34	36	31	33	28	33	36
Clear guidelines for good/evil	28	27	28	30	21	29	37
Member of religious organization	22	28	14	23	15	21	32
One true religion	21	13	25	27	15	19	31
Great confidence in church	19	15	19	24	8	16	35
Encourage faith in child	14	14	10	16	7	11	25
Weekly churchgoer	14	16	11	14	10	13	20
Member welfare charity	8	5	7	8	5	9	12
Risk life for religion	4	5	4	3	4	4	4
Average	32	32	32	34	26	32	40

Source: Abrams et al., 1985, p. 32.

many ways as a result of the Victorian attitude to sex. Rejection of premarital or extramarital sex meant that young men required the services of prostitutes or else exploited the family maid. London, it is estimated, had anything up to 100,000 prostitutes in Victoria's reign and the exploitation of servants was notorious. Nor did the notion of sex only within marriage help family life much. It probably encouraged wife-beating 'which constituted a major social problem' (Read, 1979, p. 39), with 87,000 separation orders being issued between 1897 and 1906 on this ground alone. The lack of contraception and the stress on procreation meant yet another problem: the subjection of women. As one commentator has written, 'The prospect of a lifetime of childbearing and poverty lay ahead for most girls. At the turn of the century the life expectation of a woman of 20 was 46 years. Approximately one-third of this was likely to be given to the physiological and emotional demands of childbearing and maternal care of infants' (Read, 1979, p. 219). Nor was the situation of upper-class women any different. In 1857, for example, Lady Lyttleton was warned by her doctor that, having already borne 11 children, a twelfth pregnancy would mean her death. Yet she duly became pregnant and on being asked why she had neglected to inform her husband of the medical risk involved, she replied: 'My dear, we never speak of anything so nasty [as sex]' (Read, 1979, p. 216). One suspects, therefore, that her experiences were less than 'sacramental'. It was their consequences which were to bring her closer to God.

By the 1960s, however, it was precisely the belief that morals should be based on the likely consequences rather than on the intrinsic righteousness of any act that was to form the basis of the legislation giving rise to the so-called 'permissive society'. The laws involved included the Obscene Publications Act of 1959, the Suicide Act of 1961, the Murder (Abolition of the Death Penalty) Act of 1965, the Abortion Act of 1967, the Sexual Offences Act of 1967, the Theatres Act of 1968 and the Divorce Act of 1969. The most controversial and resented of all this legislation, according to opinion poll evidence, was the reform of the law on homosexuality, which is therefore used in this chapter to highlight the debate over permissiveness.

The change of attitudes from moralism to 'causalism' has been chronicled best by Christie Davies in his book *Permissive Britain: Social Change in the Sixties and Seventies* (1975). He differentiates 'causalist' from 'utilitarian' ethics by pointing out that the causalists seem to have limited their consideration of the consequences of any legislation in two ways: first, by considering only the short-term consequences of their decisions (assuming in practice that people's moral attitudes would not be affected by them); and, secondly, by having regard to only negative utility, and ignoring positive good or happiness. Hence, for example, with regard to the first limitation, divorce was made easier to obtain, without assuming that this would alter people's attitudes to marriage; or, with regard to the second limitation, the fact that many people claimed to achieve happiness from using cannabis did not prevent the ban on the use of this drug from being enforced.

Generally speaking, the aim of the legislation was to minimize the harm, suffering, conflict or distress caused by previous legislation: hence, homosexuality was made legal, divorce made easier, capital punishment abolished and abortion made legally available. In all of these cases what counted were the consequences. MPs did not suddenly approve of homosexuality: they merely no longer saw the point of persecuting a substantial minority of the population on account of different sexual preferences; likewise, in cases where marriages had already 'irretrievably broken down' there seemed little point in refusing to allow divorce or in pinpointing a 'guilty party'. In the case of abortion reform, the arguments in a non-Catholic country, while partly centring on theological grounds, were actually won on points concerning back-street abortionists and medical and social consequences. Even the opponents of abortion used causalist arguments, insinuating, for example, that 'abortion on demand' would lead to euthanasia and mass extermination. The debate on the abolition of the death penalty followed similar lines. Points of principle were indeed discussed; yet in the end it was the belief that the death penalty was ineffective as a deterrent and that too many innocent people had been hanged already that clinched the argument for the abolitionists. Finally, with respect to censorship, the inability to get juries to convict and the tendency for the law to look ridiculous led to the relatively more liberal Obscene Publications Act of 1959 and the Theatres Act of 1968 which abolished the Lord Chamberlain's right to censor stage plays.

The fact that the permissive legislation of the 1960s was based on 'causalist' ethics should serve in itself to emphasize the important point that, had the legislation been based on 'moralist ethics', it might have been a great deal more radical. Yet parliament never sought to replace 'old' Christian values with 'new' 'permissive' ones. In Davies's words: 'Parliament was at no stage seized with a zeal for permissiveness which led it to alter eagerly all the restrictive legislation it had inherited from its predecessors' (Davies, 1975, p. 14). Indeed, the very process of reform showed this:

Parliamentary majorities were never guaranteed and despite the warm backing of Roy Jenkins as Home Secretary from 1965–67, which allowed government time to be used for the legislation, all of the reforming Acts began as private members' bills and were voted on as a matter of private conscience, not party loyalty. The moral reforms were marginal to the central direction of the government and were often seen as irrelevant by those who directed its strategy.

47

It is this range of circumstances forming a complex political conjuncture, which in large part explains the contradictory nature of many of the reforms. They were the end results of a variety of different pressures: liberal reformism, pragmatic acceptance of the need for change, eccentric libertarianism, religious, especially Roman Catholic, counter-pressure and other sustained special interest agitation or opposition, channelled through Members of Parliament. (Weeks, 1981, p. 267)

The difficulties involved in securing parliamentary majorities for the reforms help to explain two otherwise puzzling characteristics of them: first, what Weeks (1981, p. 267) refers to as their 'self-contained' nature; secondly, their limitations. Each reform had to be argued on its own merits and the pressure-group involved had to build up its own constellation of supporters. The chief concern was to obtain a parliamentary majority and not to risk alienating potential moderate supporters. The chief tactic was to identify the social problem area and to press for isolated reforms to alleviate the problem concerned.

The result, therefore, was that the reforms achieved were in fact limited ones. Homosexuals, for example, could only indulge in sex if they were over the age of 21, and if the act took place between consenting adults in private. Moreover, the law did not change when the age of majority was later lowered from 21 to 18. Again, although abortion was made available on social grounds in pregnancies of up to 28 weeks, the Act fell far short of abortion on demand. Very often the crucial issue was the medical opinion of the physician concerned.

Some topics proved too hot to handle for the legislators. For example, there was considerable debate in the 1960s and 1970s on the effect of sex and violence in films and on television. Summarizing the state of research in 1975, Davies wrote:

On both of these subjects extensive research has been carried out in America, Britain, Denmark, Italy, Australia and many other countries. The results are complex and often contradictory and the methods used often suspect but two interesting conclusions do emerge. First, the free availability of pornography seems to reduce rather than increse the number of sex crimes. The cathartic effect exceeds the incitement effect and censorship does not seem to be justified. Second, television violence does seem to result in the viewers being more violent in their everyday lives. The incitement effect exceeds the cathartic effect and the censors seem to have a good case. These are the general conclusions of the extensive research in these two areas, conclusions that point in opposite directions in the two cases. (Davies, 1975, p. 57)

Causalist legislators as a result should have censored violence and encouraged sex on television. Yet, if anything, the opposite happened, in films as well. This may well have something to do with peculiarly British attitudes towards sex; more likely, it had to do with moral uncertainties and moral confusion.

Where, then, will all this lead? To attempt to answer the question, it is necessary to examine the underlying causes of the shift in attitudes in the 1960s in the first place; thereafter, one has to review the progress, or decline, that has occurred since then. For only at the end of this process will it be possible to reach a conclusion. With regard to the underlying cause, the role of the secularization of society, as has already been pointed out, has perhaps been over-emphasized. Besides, the different churches themselves have often upheld 'permissive values'; for example, the 1963 report *Towards a Quaker View of Sex* placed 'love' at the heart of morality, rather than tradition, revelation or authority. According to this report, love, including homosexual love, could no longer 'be confined to a pattern', a viewpoint which all the other churches, except for the Roman Catholic, were subsequently to uphold, to a greater or lesser extent.

If 'secularization', therefore, cannot in itself account for the permissive society of the 1960s, what other factors should we take into account to explain the shift in values? Historians in their investigations of previous 'sexual revolutions' – in Austria or Russia for example, before 1914, in Weimar Germany in the 1920s, in the USA in the 1920s and 1960s – have tended to stress factors such as increased urbanization, increased mobility and the effect of cinema and television (for the 1920s and 1960s). All of these are considered to have been influences which frustrated the social controls associated with small-town society, religion and the extended family.

Clearly, however, other factors were at work. For example, there was the growing influence of Freudian psycho-analysis which placed man's sexual drive at the very centre of his being. In Britain, the sexual mores of the Bloomsbury group may also have been influential. Sexual research, too, was to make an impact. The famous Kinsey Reports of the 1940s were to suggest that there was a spectrum of sexuality between male and female and that most people fell somewhere in between. They discovered that more than 40 per cent of American men surveyed had had homosexual experiences, more than 30 per cent of them to the point of orgasm. Thus sexology, like Freudian psychiatry, was to lead to a generally greater open-mindedness about sex and sexuality. Medical advances, too, were to play their part in the evolution of greater tolerance of sex. Decisive here were innovations such as the sheath (used by the army in the First World War to reduce the incidence of veneral disease) and the oral contraceptive pill (freely available on the British National Health Service by 1969). Equally important, of course, was the development of salvarsan (1910) and antibiotics (after 1945) for the cure of venereal disease. By the 1960s both syphilis and gonorrhoea could be cured in a matter of weeks or even days. Sex became increasingly risk free, and with the legalisation of abortion yet another avenue of evading unwanted consequences was made available. Little wonder therefore a 'sexual revolution' was possible. Yet there were still other factors which helped to bring it about.

One was the so-called 'youth revolution' of the 1960s. This was composed of several elements: a 20 per cent increase in the number of unmarried people between the ages of 15 and 24 (the post-war baby boom); a 50 per cent increase in average real wages for adolescents since 1938; and a vast new market of 'youth' commodities (record players, cosmetics, cheap exotic clothing). Many of these commodities were advertised with a more blatant emphasis on sex, since boys and girls were reaching sexual maturity about four to five years earlier than in the previous century largely as a result of rising living standards. In Britain, however, all this led more to a change in style and attitudes rather than to a change in sexual practices. People tended to have sex earlier and girls had illegitimate babies at a slightly younger age, but this reflected physiological change rather than a revolution in sexual mores. Likewise, although venereal disease rates increased by 34 per cent, hospital admissions in general increased by 43 per cent, demonstrating the availability of more facilities rather than a change in medical patterns. Michael Schofield in his *The Sexual Problems of Young People*, published in the mid-1960s, found a general conservatism: most boys said they would marry a girl if they made her pregnant, but most boys still wanted to marry virgins; and the vast majority of Schofield's sample (boys and girls) were still virgins themselves. A Sunday Times survey of the late 1960s discovered that more than one-quarter of men and nearly two-thirds of women interviewed had been virgins when they married. Recent research also demonstrates widespread support for traditional sexual values, with solid majorities among all classes and age-groups disapproving of under-age sex, extramarital affairs, prostitution, homosexuality and abortion as table 3.2 shows.

Although by the 1970s, women's magazines were promoting concepts of femininity based on the idea that the female body was worthy of stimulation and excitation as well as motherhood and domestic bliss, the 'feminist legislation' of the late 1960s and 1970s (the Equal Pay Act, the Sex Discrimination Act) 'did little to fundamentally undermine the complex structure of female subordination' enshrined in the social security system (Weeks, 1981, p. 258). The social position of women therefore did not radically alter, save for the fact that many working-class women could now get part-time jobs. None the less, modern advertising, modern contraception, the establishment of family planning and venereal disease clinics, not to mention the lyrics and behaviour of rock 'n' roll idols, convinced conservatives that a sexual revolution was underway. The

50

Table 3.2 Percentage endorsement of traditional sex values

Item	Total sample	Social class				Age		
		ABC1	C2	DE		18–34	35–54	55+
Under-age sex unjustified	82	82	83	81		75	86	88
Extramarital affairs unjustified	74	72	75	77		68	74	83
Prostitution unjustified	70	66	71	75		61	69	88
Homosexuality unjustified	65	59	68	71		56	65	79
Abortion unjustified	60	55	60	66		54	57	70
Disapprove single parent	47	47	47	45		34	45	65
Sex needs moral rules	40	46	39	35		34	39	48
Accept ninth commandment	79	79	78	79		69	82	86
Accept sixth commandment	78	79	77	77		68	80	87
Object unmarried mothers as neighbours	3	3	4	3		1	2	8
Average	60	50	60	61		52	60	70

Source: Abrams et al., 1985, p. 34.

truth, however, seems to be that sexual behaviour changed very little.

A final point should be made here. One of the most popular slogans of the 1960s was 'make love not war', and it is a slogan which perhaps deserves some comment. Kinsey, for example, in the 1940s discovered that there had been a sexual revolution in the USA immediately after the First World War, which is borne out by American literature of the 1920s. By then, of course, many young men had been demobilized and sought release in a different life-style. Yet they may also have been positively reacting against military values. Certainly one reason why the 'sexual revolution' of the 1960s frightened many traditionally minded citizens was that it seemed to represent a set of values that challenged more than just sexual conformity. The liberation of the 1960s became closely identified in the minds of many people with political protest movements, particularly that against the war in Vietnam. Thus 'make love not war' seemed to challenge resistance to world communism and to undermine the moral fibre of the West. Young people openly despised militarism: uniforms became part of hippy dress; combat dress became casual wear. In Great Britain by the 1960s conscription had been abolished. This, of course, was to make way for a professional army backed up by nuclear weapons, a policy partly determined by Britain's economic decline. Was economic decline therefore leading to moral decline? Did the end of conscription signify the end of self-restraint among the adolescents of the country who would no longer be disciplined by British sergeant-majors? Christie Davies, for one, has argued that it was the decline of the British Empire that allowed the law on homosexuality to be reformed in the 1960s: 'While we had an empire we needed taboos against homosexuality' (Davies, 1975, p. 139). He generalizes his argument as follows:

It is curious to note that the only important countries in Europe to retain laws against homosexuality right up to the 1960s were Britain, Germany and the Soviet Union. These were also the only three European countries to create bureaucratic mass armies that were able to fight a protracted war under twentieth-century conditions and whose morale did not crack up in the process. Of these countries Britain and the Soviet Union were imperial powers with large empires to defend and Germany sought to become such a power. Germany and the Soviet Union are countries with strong militarist traditions, large conscript armies during this century and a tendency to invade their neighbours. (Davies, 1975, p. 138)

In support of his thesis that militaristic societies are both sexually aggressive and homophobic, Davies cites the evidence of a Danish sociologist. (Denmark became notorious for sexual promiscuity during the 1960s.)

> We are not puritans in this country. Our life has been too easy since we stopped going on raids all over Europe in the Viking days. Denmark has not been involved in any major war for the last two centuries. World War II brought a rapid occupation that in itself prevented much show of martial spirit. This has given the military tradition very unfavourable conditions for many years: a rather important point since a military society generally has a high degree of sexual stratification, men being normally considered superior to women. (Davies, 1975, pp. 138–9)

Does the breakdown of an imperial past therefore explain the rise of the permissive society in Great Britain? Surely not. Davies, like many British historians, simply loses his way when he attempts to look for parallels abroad. In the late nineteenth century, at the height of Empire, neither France nor Russia, our main imperial rivals, had laws against homosexuals. Austria–Hungary, which did not boast much of a military tradition, did. Moreover, the tightening up of the British law in 1885 came about not as a result of militarist apprehensions, but as a by-product of a campaign against child prostitution. Finally, although homosexuality is today generally legal in Western Europe, conscription is also general. There is no straightforward relationship therefore between militarism and the legalization of homosexual acts. A general point which can perhaps be made is that military values do not normally include tolerance. Tolerance of sexual freedom, on the other hand, has traditionally depended on many factors – political, economic, social, religious and cultural – quite apart from the military one.

If we can now explain the sexual revolution and how it arose by the 1960s, what view should we take of how far it has gone and how we should react to it? As has been seen, although it was very limited in practice, it none the less seemed to many people to threaten the very moral fibre of Western society. Some left-wingers did indeed attempt to exploit it. Herbert Marcuse, for example, in his best-selling books *Eros and Civilization* and *One Dimensional Man*, tried to establish a link between capitalism and eroticism (suppressed during the early phases of capitalism in favour of the work ethic, necessary in the latest one to promote consumerism), but was unconvincing in his attempts to mobilize minority groups to overthrow the system. The work of William Reich, the 'sexual radical' of the inter-war period, also achieved some influence. In the Centre, the view taken was that the permissive society, in Roy Jenkins's famous phrase, was really the 'civilized society'. This reflected the fact that most of the reforms of the late 1960s had indeed been limited ones.

On the Right, however, resistance to 'permissiveness' was organized by evangelical Christians around such bodies as the National Viewers' and Listeners' Association and the Festival of Light. Their main spokesmen were Mrs Mary Whitehouse, Lord Longford and Malcolm Muggeridge, their main quarry the Director General of the BBC between 1960 and 1969, Sir Hugh Carleton Greene, who in turn damned them as 'dangerous to the whole quality of life in this country ... [to] freedom, tolerance, adventure' (quoted in Tracey and Morrison, 1979, p. 199). Mrs Whitehouse and her allies attempted to 'clean up television', film and the press by protests to the BBC and the IBA; legal challenges against *Gay News*, *Oz* magazine, the *Little Red Schoolbook*, the *International Times* and the Swedish film *More about the Language of Love*; and campaigns against modern sex education in schools. Also involved was support for the Society for the Protection of the Unborn Child which almost succeeded in 1980 in restricting the abortion laws; as well as successful pressure to do away with sex-shop window displays; and the introduction of a Protection of Children Bill (1978) which produced a law designed to stop the use of children in pornography.

Mrs Whitehouse, however, has not been satisfied with the results of her campaigns. Television, she maintains, still shows too much sex and violence, while the permissive legislation of the 1960s has led to widespread divorce (by 1979 there was one divorce for every three marriages), a million legal abortions by 1980, and a feminist movement which demands not merely the right to equal pay but free access to birth control, abortion on demand, free 24-hour nursery provision and an end to gender roles and thus to the traditional norms of heterosexuality. Worst of all, for Mrs Whitehouse, the 1970s saw the birth in London of a Gay Liberation Front, as well as a Campaign for Homosexual Equality which promoted telephone help-lines, gay bars, gay newspapers and gay professional groups. There is now therefore a 'gay community', not merely a 'sub-culture'.

What, then, does all this mean? Certainly, it has meant a polarization of attitudes in the 1980s between those who wish to reverse the reforms of the 1960s and those who wish to extend the rather limited advances of that 'permissive decade'. Most probably the reformers will win the day and for the following reasons: first, even among committed Christians, not all, perhaps not even a majority, are committed to fundamentalist interpretations of the Bible; secondly, the Church itself has taken an increasingly permissive view of what the Bible teaches; thirdly, despite changes in values, the majority of people still adhere to monogamous, heterosexual relationships, still get married, still marry in church, so that the threat to traditional values is often considered to be remote; fourthly, the younger generation and probably the majority of the population as a whole have now accepted the 'sexual revolution' – at least as far as others are concerned. Feminism is already old hat; Quentin

Crisp has become an accepted television personality; pop stars like Elton John and Boy George can admit to being bisexual. Even the scare over AIDS has not led to a general witch-hunt against the gay community.

The major reason for this is the limited measure of change that has, in fact, occurred in British society. Take marriage, for example. Despite the increase in the divorce rate and in one-parent families (although only 2.2 per cent of all families in 1981 were headed by unmarried mothers), marriage has never been more popular. The proportion of married women per 1,000 women during this century has risen continuously: from 340 in 1901 to 412 in 1931 to 487 in 1951 to 491 in 1979 (Mount, 1982, Appendix Table No. 3, p. 259). In 1978 it was found that 95 per cent of women and 91 per cent of men were married by the age of 40. Even divorce does not put people off: by 1982 no less than 30 per cent of all marriages were re-marriages, with roughly half of all divorced people remarrying, mostly within a year of their divorce (Abrams et al., 1985, pp. 110–11). The Values Survey for Great Britain, published in 1985, found that 84 per cent disagreed with the statement that 'marriage is an outdated institution' and only 1.6 per cent admitted to 'living as married' (Abrams et al., 1985, p. 114). True, various surveys have discovered that between 5 and 10 per cent of couples cohabit *before marriage* but the point to note is that cohabitation is nowadays usually a *premarital* practice. As the Values Survey concludes:

> It is not the fact of marriage that is being questioned, but rather the quality of married life ... Individuals do not divorce because marriage has become unimportant to them, but it has become so important to them that they have no tolerance for the less than completely successful marital arrangement ... although increasing numbers of people are rejecting specific marriage partners, the institution of marriage is not threatened and this is underlined by the high rate of remarriage following divorce. (Abrams et al., 1985, p. 144)

This conclusion has been reinforced by the work of John Gillis whose book, *For Better or Worse: British Marriages 1600 to the Present*, has described the contemporary marriage process as being strikingly similar to that of the sixteenth and seventeenth centuries, with couples forming 'little marriages', that is to say cohabiting, before their 'big weddings'. This practice (which often never reached the 'big wedding' stage) was made illegal by the Hardwicke Act of 1753 and led to the very high illegitimacy rates of early Victorian England. It was not until the early twentieth century that marriage became the norm for most people. However, by the 1950s and 1960s never had so many married so elaborately and so conventionally. Taking the story up to the present, Gillis argues:

55

Then in the 1970s things came apart. The incidence of co-habitation rose rapidly, premarital pregnancy increased and illegitimacy began to approach levels similar to those of the early Victorian period. It seemed to many that marriage itself was under siege, as the age of newlyweds rose for the first time in fifty years, and more and more people seemed to be avoiding nuptiality altogether. However, it was not so much marriage itself but the preliminaries that were changing. Couples were postponing rather than abandoning formal marriage. Those who elected to live together were doing so for relatively brief periods; when they did marry their preference was the big wedding ... In the past, little weddings served the needs of those who could not meet society's requirements for full marriage. Today the high standard symbolised by the rites of the large wedding is the reason many postpone marriage. What the availability of land and trade were to the people of the 16th and 17th centuries, consumer durables and a secure career are to the current generation ... It is little wonder that so many people prefer a little wedding until they can gather the resources for a big one. Despite all the talk of a breakdown of morality, those who choose to live together before marriage are honouring rather than defying society's standards and traditions. (Gillis, *New Society*, 18 July 1986, p. 11)

The gay community provides another example of limited change, although its status, it can be argued, is a highly significant one. If one takes the view that the permissive society represents not decadence but an important extension of individual freedoms – indeed, it has been convincingly argued by Simon Karlinsky (1984) that the word 'decadence' is merely a pejorative term for individual freedom – then the status of homosexuals in society may well represent the litmus test of social tolerance.

Despite certain social changes since the 1960s, British society, we can conclude, has hardly suffered any 'moral collapse'. Most people have become tolerant in their attitudes to sexual behaviour, and women have won a limited measure of sexual freedom and independence. However, most changes have taken place in attitudes and fashions rather than in behaviour. And the limited change in behaviour that has occurred has taken place in the face of a huge amount of articulated outrage on the part of fundamentalist Christians. The truth may be rather that instead of a moral collapse the permissiveness of the 1960s represented only a small increase in individual freedom and that in this important area a great deal more remains to be done.

Crime

It is commonly believed that modern Britain is more crime-ridden than ever before, that law and order is in danger of breaking down and that women in particular cannot walk abroad for fear of being mugged or raped. Riots in many of the major English cities have reinforced this perception. Has Britain therefore declined into a pit of criminality? At least in comparison with other countries, this does not appear to be the case. Crime rates, as assessed by the National Police Agency of Japan for 1983, give the figures for various crimes

Table 3.3   Crimes committed per 100,000 population in different countries

	Homicide	Forcible rape	Robbery
USA	8.3	38.7	213.8
West Germany	4.5	11.0	48.1
France	5.0	5.2	93.6
England and Wales	2.8	8.8	44.6
Japan	1.6	1.7	1.9

Source: National Police Agency of Japan, given in *The Economist*, 14–20 December 1985.

committed per 100,000 inhabitants shown in Table 3.3. From these statistics, it will be seen that compared with other countries (especially in the West) Britain does not appear to be as sunk in criminality as her neighbours. Yet there appears, none the less, to have been a significant increase in crime in Britain in the course of this century. According to one source (Bell, 1962), the number of indictable crimes in England and Wales in 1900 was about 80,000; in London alone it was about 1,800. In 1938 the comparable totals were 283,220 and 95,280. By 1959 the figures for 1900 had multiplied eightfold to 675,626. According to another source (Dahrendorf, 1985), crime in Britain since the 1960s has tripled or quadrupled with respect to violent crime and theft. What conclusions, therefore, can be drawn from these figures?

According to some experts, the proper conclusion to draw is that the figures are simply misleading. In their view, Britain is a relatively less violent society than it was a century ago. Thus, *The Economist* (1 March 1986, p. 27), reviewing *Violent Disorders in Twentieth Century Britain* by E. G. Dunning, P. Murphy, T. Newburr and I. Waddington (University of Leicester Press, 1986) headlined its article: 'A peaceable people', arguing that 'Many people think that Britain is more violent and nastier than ever before. They are probably wrong.' The review pointed out that the increased number of burglaries recorded by the police between 1972 and 1981 (60 per cent) did not tally with the results obtained from the General Household Surveys (closer to 10 per cent). It also argued: 'In absolute terms, homicide has indeed become much more common over the years. But so have people: after adjusting the murder rate for population increases, it turns out that the risk of being a murder victim is now less than it was a hundred years ago. In the early 1980s, a Briton's chance of being murdered was about 25 per cent lower than it was in the 1860s.' The Leicester sociologists took their statistics from reports between 1900 and 1975 in the *Leicester Mercury*. They discovered that industrial violence had 'declined dramatically' in the course of the century, that there had been a downward trend in political violence, that community violence was down and that the only upward trend was to be found in violence associated with sport and leisure. It may be that the newspaper which provided their source materials had been guilty of under-reporting violence as the century wore on. The authors, however, were of the opinion that its style had in fact become more sensationalist so that if anything it was even more inclined to report violence. Hence their surprise at the decline in the number of incidents reported, especially since during the same period the British population had grown by 46 per cent. Their results are summarized in figure 3.1.

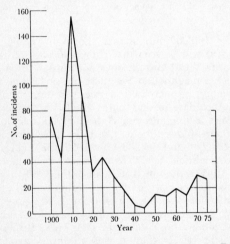

Figure 3.1.   Reported rate of violent disturbances in England, Wales and Scotland, 1900–75 (from E. G. Dunning, P. Murphy, T. Newburn, and I. Waddington, *Violent Disorders in Twentieth Century Britain*. University of Leicester, 1986.)

If such figures are correct and Britain is now, in fact, a relatively more law-abiding country than in the past, this might explain the extremely conservative attitudes on crime detected by the British Values Survey. According to this, 83 per cent disapproved of any

Table 3.4 Percentage endorsement of traditional property values

Item	Total sample	Social class			Age		
		ABC1	C2	DE	18–34	35–54	55+
Would never damage property	96	96	95	97	91	99	99
Would never use violence	95	95	96	95	91	97	99
Joy-riding unjustified	88	88	88	87	86	88	89
Accepting bribes unjustified	84	85	82	83	81	85	87
Threatening non-strikers unjustified	83	84	82	82	79	84	87
Claiming unentitled benefit unjustified	83	83	84	81	79	86	86
Buying stolen goods unjustified	81	82	80	81	75	83	87
Avoiding fares unjustified	79	80	80	78	72	82	86
Encourage honesty in children	78	79	76	80	77	76	79
Failing to report accidental damage unjustified	76	78	75	76	70	76	85
Keeping money found unjustified	76	76	75	76	68	82	84
Cheating on tax returns unjustified	73	74	73	72	67	73	81
Lying in own interest unjustified	72	72	72	74	68	69	78
Encourage thrift in children	9	6	10	16	3	11	15
Average	77	77	76	77	72	78	82

Source: Abrams et al., 1985, p. 43.

justification for taking marijuana, 84 per cent condemned terrorism, 82 per cent condemned assassination and 82 per cent said fighting the police was unjustified (Abrams et al., 1985, pp. 38, 40). Overwhelmingly traditional attitudes towards property values were also recorded as table 3.4 demonstrates.

Some people – perhaps many – will probably remain sceptical of such arguments. They should, however, retain an open mind and try to understand the difficulties facing anyone who undertakes to examine the problems involved, particularly since the investigator is not only 'uncertain how much of any type of conduct is being reported and recorded but also, since criminal statistics at present use legal definitions as the basis of subdivisions, he must recognise that even what is recorded under the same heading is a very mixed bag' (Walker, 1965. p. 18). Some basic points have to be borne in mind from the outset. First, the official figures may give a misleading impression of what is actually happening either by exaggerating or underplaying the real trends. For example, table 3.5 demonstrates how the murder rate looked more stable than events actually warranted between 1930 and 1961.

Table 3.5 Annual average number of reported offences per million inhabitants aged eight or older in England and Wales

Years	Murder	Attempted murder	Indictable woundings
1930–9	3.6	2.2	46
1950–4	3.7	4.0	152
1955–9	4.2	4.2	243
1960–1	4.4	4.8	372

Source: Walker, 1965, p. 19.

Table 3.5 shows that murder as a crime increased by only 20 per cent over the period concerned. However, 'recorded attempts successful and unsuccessful' (Walker, 1965, p. 19) had increased by some 60 per cent over the same period. In other words, it was probably only a mixture of luck and medical skills that had kept the rate of increase in the murder rate relatively low.

The following description of the background to the Wolfenden Committee Report of 1957, on the other hand, demonstrates how official figures can be exaggerated by other factors:

There was nothing surprising in prostitution and (male) homosexuality offences being seen as a common subject for investigation. Not only had they been historically intertwined in legal practice but both were seen as evidence of a common problem: a decline in moral standards. The most widely offered evidence for this was provided by the figures for prosecutions. In the case of street offences these had risen from around an annual average of 2,000 in the early years of the war to over 10,000 by 1952 and to almost 12,000 by 1955. The number of indictable male homosexual offences increased five-fold in the same period. In 1938 there were 134 cases of sodomy and bestiality known to the police in England and Wales; in 1952, 670; and in 1954, 1043. For indecent assault the increase was from 822 cases in 1938 to 3,305 in 1953, while for 'gross indecency' (the Labouchère offence) the rise was from 316 in 1938 to 2,322 in 1955. *Despite the dramatic rises, however, the Wolfenden Committee found little evidence that the incidence of those offences was actually increasing, though there was possibly a greater visibility of prostitution. The main factor involved was undoubtedly an increase of police zeal in hunting out offenders* and this was more evident in one or two metropolitan areas than throughout the country as a whole. The stepping up of the purge of homosexuals and prostitutes appears to have coincided with the appointment of Sir Theobald Matthew, an ardent Roman Catholic, as Director of Public Prosecutions in 1944. The prosecutions reached a new peak in London in late 1953 following the appointment of a new Metropolitan Police Commissioner, Sir John Nott-Bower, under the aegis of a fervently anti-homosexual and moralistic Home Secretary, Sir David Maxwell-Fyffe. (Weeks, 1981, pp. 239–40, my italics)

Walker, too, has commented on how the rate of offences rose and fell as the committee was first appointed and then reported: 'The most probable explanation is that the report led to a less censorious attitude on the part of both public and police' (Walker, 1965, p. 26). Thus the first point to remember when considering crime rates is that the official statistics may or may not reflect what is actually happening.

The second point to note is that the vast majority of crimes are not reported and never have been. (One might add, too, that of those reported the great majority are never solved and never will be.) Different authorities suggest different figures for the percentage of crimes reported to the police: 5, 10, 15, 20, 25 per cent. There is general agreement, however, that most crime goes unreported and for a variety of reasons: family pride or shame; mistrust of the police; little expectation of any remedy being found; sympathy or pity for the criminal involved. The result is that any increase in the reporting of crime will serve to increase the 'crime rate'. Hence, to quote Walker again:

We have only to suppose that in pre-war England 10 per cent of minor indictable assaults were reported, and that by the nineteen-sixties 25 per cent were reported, to see how the statistics would show an apparent increase of 250 per cent. We cannot of course dismiss the whole of the apparent increase this way: almost certainly some of it reflects a real trend. But equally certainly the real trend is not nearly as spectacular as the statistics make it seem. (Walker, 1965, p. 20)

Are there factors, therefore, that would help to explain the figures in table 3.6 in terms of increased reporting of crime?

There are a number of suggestions that have been made. First, it is useful to consider how the police record crime. One criminologist has suggested with regard to crimes of violence, for example, that between 1938 and 1960 changes in recording methods by the police could have caused an apparent increase in crime of 13 per cent alone (Walker, 1965, p. 20). In 1986, the *Observer* reported that many policemen were coming forward to support allegations that the police were 'faking their statistics' or 'cooking the books' (reports of 13 and 20 July by Home Affairs correspondent, Nick Davies). According to these sources: 'Scores of fictitious crimes [had] been invented and then "solved" with false confessions, to bolster the crime figures.' The report of 20 July ran: 'The detectives, who come from various different forces, say that perversion of the course of justice in order to boost the crime figures is commonplace in forces throughout England and Wales.' One detective with more than 20 years' experience was quoted as saying: 'The police authority sit there telling us we are doing a wonderful job, when we're not. The real truth is that the figures are fixed to keep the local politicians off the chief constable's back. I think we should tell the truth.' Such allegations may well explain the discrepancies between the police statistics and the findings of the General Household Surveys regarding burglaries mentioned above.

A second reason why more crime might have been reported may be attributable to a change in attitudes. It may be that whereas, especially in certain areas, crime was previously 'kept within the family', this is no longer a norm which is respected. Increased social mobility, the breakdown of the extended family, changing attitudes towards family life, plus the influence of newspapers and television, may all play a part here. The end result may be a greater willingness to report crime. Certainly there are greater opportunities: the introduction of the 999 telephone system in 1937, plus the post-war expansion of the telephone network, means that there is now little difficulty or even effort required in contacting the police. More recently, television programmes such as *Crime Watch* or *Police Watch* have created added inducements. It is even possible that the added publicity given to rape and other sexual crimes has led to the rise in the figures for rapes. Has rape become more common or are women nowadays simply more willing to come forward and discuss

Table 3.6 Annual average number of reported property and rape offences per million inhabitants aged eight or older in England and Wales

Years	Larceny	Burglary	Robbery	Fraud	Rape and indecent assault
1930–9	4441(100)	1086(100)	6(100)	432(100)	60(100)
1950–4	8320	2359	24	702	198
1955–9	9267	2681	33	686	226
1960–1	12631(284)	3915(278)	54(900)	937(217)	248(414)

Figures in brackets represent percentage increase if 1930 = 100.
Source: Walker, 1965, pp. 25, 28.

their ordeals? Certainly press coverage of rape and other sexual crimes has been spectacular:

> A recent survey of Scottish newspapers showed that as a proportion of crimes mentioned, offences involving sex were over-represented numerically fourteen times (and by area of print seventeen times) in comparison with the actual incidence of these offences among officially recorded crimes ... Newspaper editors seem to be convinced that the public wants to read as much as it can about sex and that sex offences will therefore always be news and will always sell copies. We are in no position to judge whether that conviction is always well-founded, but it undoubtedly results in sex offences receiving far greater coverage in the public prints than their frequency alone – as a proportion of crime in general or even of serious crime – would warrant. (Howard League Report, 1985, pp. 61–2)

Finally, with regard to incentives to report, it should be remembered that almost all insurance companies now require claimants to report their losses, however trivial, to the police before they can submit claims for reimbursement. This alone must boost the crime figures considerably since many people would otherwise not bother to contact the police.

Some, perhaps even a considerable proportion, of the increase in crime in modern Britain can therefore be accounted for in purely statistical terms. Moreover, while discussing the figures relating to murder up to 1961, Walker has further words of comfort:

> When it is realised that murders in Britain are so few – about four per million inhabitants every year – and that the sane murderer is responsible for less than a third of them, it becomes clear how rare a person he is. His final act seems to be premeditated but more often to be the outcome either of a sudden quarrel or of a situation in which he is surprised or resisted in the course of committing a robbery or burglary. (Walker, 1965, p. 21)

Murder, in fact, in 1961 was 'numerically as insignificant in the criminal statistics as death from anthrax was among this country's infectious diseases' (Walker, 1965, p. 36).

The figures for offences coming before the English courts in 1961 are shown in table 3.7. Walker commented on this list of figures:

> It is dominated by traffic offences, which account for nearly two out of three cases. Of the remaining third, one-third consists of 'property offences' to which we ought probably to add revenue evasions and most railway offences as repre-

Table 3.7   Percentage of offences coming before the English courts in 1961

Offence	%
Traffic	61.3
Breaking and entering (3.2); receiving (0.8); and larceny (9.3)	13.3
Drunkenness	7.0
Murder (0.001) and other non-sexual violence (1.999)	2.0
Sexual offences	1.0
Revenue evasions	2.5
Railway offences	1.8
Breaches of local bye-laws and similar regulations	2.2
Malicious damage to property	1.6
Miscellaneous	7.3
Total (1,152,397)	100.0

Source: Walker, 1965, p. 37.

senting other forms of dishonesty. Next in numbers are sexual offenders. It is essential however to remind ourselves that if all offences of every kind were conscientiously reported to the police and successfully prosecuted the proportions would almost certainly differ in two respects. Property offenders – who in this statistically imperfect world so often escape detection – would dominate the picture even more and all the unknown number of unreported sexual offences would greatly add to that 1 per cent. In this corrected perspective, violence would appear even more insignificant. (Walker, 1965, p. 36)

Yet since 1961, as has been seen, the crime rate has more than quadrupled for crimes of violence. Has this been due to changes in recording methods by the police? By a greater readiness on the part of the public to report crime? To an unknown degree the answer is almost certainly yes. But if this is only part of the answer what other factors exist which could account for the increase in crime?

One answer is the baby boom or rather the rising proportion of young people among the population in the post-war period. Statistics show that it is boys in their last year of school who are responsible for most petty theft and that it is the young adult male of about 20 who is most likely to commit a crime of violence. One report carried out in the 1960s (quoted in Walker, 1965, p. 20) showed that the age-group most given to violence was that of 'young adults' between 17 and 21, with 'young persons' between 14 and 17 a bad second. Another study (quoted in Walker, 1965, pp. 36–7) which was conducted in the 1960s into the careers of 2,402 boys born in Britain in the first week of March 1946, who were traceable and still living in Britain, discovered that, by their 17th birthday in 1963, 8 per cent of them had already been found guilty of indictable offences and another 4 per cent had been found guilty of or cautioned for non-indictable offences, a total of one in every eight boys. Indirect calculations then suggested that after their 17th birthday a further 6 per cent of these males would be indicted for an offence, producing an adult population in which perhaps one in seven had a criminal record. Indeed, during the 1960s, out of every 38 persons summoned for jury service at the Old Bailey four certainly and nine probably had convictions serious enough to be recorded in the Criminal Record Office (Walker, 1965, p. 38). And today, according to the 1986 *Social Trends*, no less than one-third of the under-30 population has a criminal record (not including driving offences).

The situation with regard to youth has recently been described by Ralf Dahrendorf (1985) as 'shocking':

In all modern societies young people account for by far the major part of all crimes, and notably serious crimes including homicide, rape, assault and robbery. The facts are shocking from any point of view. People under twenty-one account for something like half of those found guilty of the traditional crimes ... In England boys are up to ten times as likely to be dealt with for criminal offence as full grown men and in America, similarly, the population aged fourteen to twenty-four is the group from which most criminals are drawn. In England and Wales, no fewer than eight per cent of all 14 to 16 year olds were found guilty of or cautioned for serious offences in one single year (1978). By contrast fewer than one-third of one per cent of all those who are 50 years old and older were found guilty of such offences. Moreover, the rate for older men has not changed much over the years, whereas among the young there has been a major increase. For example in England and Wales the rate of serious crimes among 14 to 16 year olds was one third of what it is today in the late 1960s. (Dahrendorf, 1985, p. 30)

It should be pointed out, however, that the role of youth in crime is hardly new. Josephine Bell, a writer of detective stories, in her survey *Crime in our Time* (1962) mentions 'a particularly astute lecture' given by a psychologist in 1937 in which it was stated that in 30–40 per cent of arrests for indictable offences the culprits were under 21 years of age. Of those, two-thirds were under seventeen. Thus recent trends were already visible before the war.

What then is the explanation? According to Miss Bell (1962, p. 232), the root of the problem is the failure of modern adult society to socialize the natural energies of 'modern rebellious healthy irreverent urban youth', the majority of whom are not naturally delinquent:

> In stressing their badness or alternately putting forward exclusively the psychological angle people forget the *normal* unpleasantness and aggression of the human race. Throwing bricks and other missiles at trains is a mischievous, dangerous pastime. Children who do it have never been taught to forego their hunting instinct where it might hurt other people. But they are not inherently *bad* only *natural* but untrained and their aim is all too often accurate and shows considerable skill. (Bell, 1962, pp. 231–2)

For Miss Bell it is the first five years of a child's life that count:

> The crux of the matter there is parental care. For too long and in too many ways parental responsibility has been undermined and supplanted. Children must be accepted for what they are, immature human beings, demanding rightly for their own survival, a maximum of care and love in infancy, a maximum of thoughtful training, until bodily functions and appetites become regulated habits, social behaviour fits into a normal happy pattern and the child is free to develop his individual preferences and activities without injuring himself or others. He cannot do this if his parents are themselves delinquent, selfish, immoral, vicious or merely indifferent. (Bell, 1962, p. 231)

'Crime', according to Miss Bell, is really the result of 'misplaced, persisting infantilism' summed up in the attitude, 'I must have what I want and do what I like, or else!' (Bell, 1962, p. 59). Consequently, she interprets the post-war crime figures as two crime waves both largely involving young people. The first occurred between 1948 and 1953 and appeared to die off by 1955. The second began in 1958 and was still continuing in 1962 when her book was published. Characteristically, however, both crime waves could be ascribed to the abnormal childhoods of the young people involved. The first group (involved as teenagers in the crime wave between 1948 and 1953) had had their earlier childhood disrupted by the Second World War, when fathers were conscripted, mothers forced to work, the children themselves often evacuated to strange surroundings. The result was delinquent teenagers later on. The teenagers of the late fifties and early sixties fared no better:

> These young criminals were born in the war and spent their earliest lives in chaotic conditions or during the first stirrings

67

of the social revolution that followed. They missed real parental care and love. Their mothers were out working, preoccupied as well by anxiety or grief. Later a totally unknown man, their father, arrived in the home. He too was unused to domesticity, trained recently in violence, reacting against his army life of discipline, danger, hardship and horror. His children resented his presence; their jealousy was even more pronounced than is usual in young children. They developed a bitter antagonism to authority and particularly to parental authority. (Bell, 1962, p. 226)

Miss Bell also blamed crime on many other factors: 'the new greediness born of prosperity', the media, advertising, lack of proper education, including moral education. But her main point was the need for parents to train their children in the first five years of infancy and to channel young energies along healthy, socially acceptable paths.

Today, other points would have to be made. First, there are a great many more objects around to steal – more cars, more stereo sets, more portable goods of all sorts. As Walker puts it, 'the affluent society is a society of opportunity which includes the dishonest as well as the industrious amongst its beneficiaries' (1965, p. 28). Moreover, with ubiquitous advertising – on radio and television, in newspapers and magazines, in shops and on hoardings – the desire for material goods is constantly stimulated. And some people at least must reach the obvious conclusion that the only way to acquire these goods is through crime, especially when, despite all the extra resources recently devoted to law and order, the crime detection rate remains abysmally low. Perhaps the wonder is that so many citizens still obey as many laws as they do.

A second major factor involved in recent crime is drugs. Dealing in drugs is, of course, itself a crime but the drugs racket has notorious secondary effects. By making addicts of its victims, it forces them to commit other crimes in order to maintain their own addiction. It also undermines the support of young people for the police since the latter is involved in confiscating 'soft drugs' which many young people regard as no more or less harmful than alcohol. Indeed, among certain sections of the community (for example, among Rastafarian West Indians) soft drugs form an important part of the local culture. (For a useful survey of the latest research into the links between drugs and crime, see the *Sunday Times* News in Focus Report of 13 July 1986 entitled 'Smack, Crack, Crime, Drugs Panic: Reality and Myth'.)

A difficult question regarding law and order is whether immigration into Britain, especially black immigration, has been a factor in the rising crime rates of the past three decades. The Brixton police, after all, were severely criticized only a few years ago for publishing figures which appeared to demonstrate that the majority of violent street crime in that borough was committed by blacks. There are certainly many whites in Britain who assume that most urban crime is caused by blacks. This cannot possibly be true, of course, although it may be true that blacks are over-represented in the criminal statistics, if such statistics exist on a racial basis. Yet this would not be surprising given the higher proportion of young people among the black population, the number of unskilled or unemployed males in it, and the relative instability of black marriages. It would, indeed, be in line with everything we know about crime, black or white. If drugs now also form an integral part of black youth culture, then this impression is merely reinforced. There is no racial factor involved. Blacks are not over-represented (if this is in fact true) because they are black, but because they are more likely to be young, poor and undisciplined.

If the influence of immigration on crime is difficult to assess, the significance of the urban riots of 1981 and 1985 is no easier to measure. Are they to be considered part of a hallowed British tradition – the Gordon Riots, the Chartist Riots, Captain Swing etc. – or as part of a post-war history that includes rioting in Northern Ireland, football hooliganism, picket-line violence during the miners' strike of 1984 and racial violence as in Notting Hill in 1958? Or are these riots symptomatic of something else? Certainly, there has been a remarkable reluctance to classify them as race riots, despite the fact that most of the rioters appear to have been black and despite the fact too that there have been no similar riots in cities like Glasgow or Dundee which, although equally affected by the recession and by government policy, have no black populations crowded into particular areas. Liberal opinion instead has chosen to focus on the breakdown of relations between police forces and their 'local communities'. Yet, although there can be no denying that a great deal of recent research (some of it commissioned by the police itself) has demonstrated the inadequacies of contemporary police forces and methods, the following question must still surely be posed: if the black community feels it has to riot, to make a point, might it not be advisable to listen to it, even if only to explain later why that point may have to be rejected? The point, however, may be a large and unnerving one. It may indeed be one that challenges government and society not merely to spend more money but to re-examine fundamental attitudes and prejudices. Deafness should be superseded by debate.

The debate, if it should begin, will be conducted in terms of basic beliefs about the nature of man. Those who believe that man is basically good (following the tradition of Rousseau or the contemporary German sociologist, Habermas) will call for fewer restraints on social behaviour, more 'reasonable' laws, greater tolerance and greater public spending on social welfare and education. Their opponents, following the tradition of Hobbes, and seeing man as intrinsically anarchic and selfish, will call for greater restraints,

69

harsher penalties and public support for the state, the law and the family – not merely for negative reasons (to control man's selfish nature) but to conserve cultural achievements (state organizations, family structures, legal frameworks) which are worth preserving. In between will be liberals, like Dahrendorf who, in his recent Hamlyn Lectures, has tried to open this debate. His model in his examination of 'law and order', however, is neither Rousseau or Hobbes, but the German liberal Kant, who desired to exploit 'man's unsocial sociability' for the common good. Like Locke and Hume, Kant saw that man was both good and bad. The liberal response therefore, like that of Miss Bell's as we saw earlier) is to accept natural instincts but to channel and control them.

The instrument for doing so, according to Dahrendorf, should be the social contract. This he defines as 'the unspoken agreement to abide by certain elementary norms and accept the monopoly of violence on the part of a common power set up to protect these norms' (Dahrendorf, 1985, p. 89). Crucially, however, these norms must include an acceptance of the rule of law. Moreover, the law should be seen as something absolute and should not be confused with economics. Hence it is wrong, he says, to refer to the 'right to work' or the 'right to a clean environment' when rights can only be discussed in terms of law. Likewise, there can be no case for discussing poverty as 'a violation of human rights'. This is not merely linguistically confusing but is a deliberately deceptive attempt to remove issues from the relative sphere of economics to the absolute sphere of law. For these issues are not truly legal ones at all: no court can abolish unemployment or end poverty. The trouble is that confusion in theory leads to confusion in practice and once the law is seen as relative this leads to further practices which undermine its value (plea-bargaining, mitigating circumstances) and 'no-go areas') both territorial in terms of ghetto areas, schools and universities and metaphorical in terms of the the 'black economy' in which the law also ceases to operate. In Dahrendorf's words 'the economic approach to sanctions removes their normative character, establishes impurity as desirable and thereby destroys the normative structure of society', whereas norms are vital to a healthy society: 'the stronger the mores, the more effective the laws tend to be' (Dahrendorf, 1985, p. 70).

For Dahrendorf, however, belief in the absolute nature of the law is only one-half of the social contract. The other is a renewed commitment to the welfare state as an integral part of the modern state. The latter, for Dahrendorf, is based on three components – civil rights (or equality before the law); universal suffrage; and social welfare (the right of everyone to a minimum income irrespective of their value in the market place). The welfare state, however, now faces serious problems. In the first place, it has not eliminated poverty: the costs of providing modern medicine and education have risen; so too have public salaries; growth has slowed down enormously; definitions of poverty have altered; and new taxes do not necessarily provide a great deal of extra revenue. Worse still, the welfare state has given rise to great bureaucracies so that many people get back only what they put in minus the administrative costs; many others feel that they get cheated altogether. The result is that these bureaucracies add to social friction as well as to social welfare, and with recent 'cuts' this friction has increased.

In Dahrendorf's view the welfare state has now not merely reached an impasse in its development but positively fails to keep about 10 per cent of the population above the poverty level – most noticeably the low paid, the disabled and single-parent families. The long-term unemployed, he believes, will soon add another 10 per cent of the population to this 'under-class' (the American term) or *Lumpenproletariat* as·Marx called it. If Britain's blacks and untrained youth are added, then presumably Britain is heading for what the Germans already refer to as the 'two-thirds society', where those in work or otherwise provided for no longer need a large part of their fellow-citizens to sustain them or their society. It is only, however, when the under-class indulges in riots or in random attacks on property and person that the majority class reacts – and not usually with generosity. It is then, says Dahrendorf, that the alarm bells of legitimacy begin to ring:

> If citizenship turns out to divide rather than unite, it has lost its force. More than that the very assumptions of the official society of its norms and sanctions and structures of authority are in jeopardy. This is what the struggle for the social contract means. It is not only a running battle with the police, but a struggle with everything that the majority stands for. Only the struggle has all the disturbing qualities of guerrilla warfare. The issue is clear enough: it is the social contract: but all the traditional methods of coping with conflict – trade unions and wage bargaining, political parties, elections and parliamentary debates – must fail. (Dahrendorf, 1985, p. 109)

Before we reach that stage Dahrendorf's solution is twofold: to strengthen the 'spirit of the laws' by upholding law as an absolute value; but in return for this (and basically this is his social contract, although he lacks the courage to say so) to reform or extend the welfare state so that it can truly provide for the 'excluded'. No doubt this would require a great deal of extra money but this is not a matter he chooses to discuss.

Is Dahrendorf right? Recent research on football hooligans, for example, has shown them to be employed, fashionably dressed (to mislead the police), able to travel to matches abroad but imbued with outdated 'masculine' and patriotic ideas that lead them to indulge in violence. They are certainly no part of the under-class that Dahrendorf describes. Yet football hooligans, muggers, urban rioters, the disabled and the long-term unemployed are all lumped together by him. Is this a helpful analysis?

Another question he avoids, although it has been asked of late, is to what extent the welfare state has itself been responsible for the attitudes and crimes which he condemns? Has it helped to destroy the work ethic? Has it given rise to a 'something for nothing' attitude? Has it not in fact encouraged precisely that 'relative view' of social conditions and the rule of law which he condemns? If poverty justifies state aid, does it not also justify theft if that aid is considered insufficient? Professor Dahrendorf's liberalism should not be accepted uncritically. Yet before we go on to discuss the impact of the welfare state, let us try to conclude this section on crime.

It would seem that although crime is rising in Britain, some (possibly a considerable) part of this rise may well be due to changes in police reporting methods and to a greater readiness to report crime. The crime rate is still not as high as in France, Germany or the USA. Much of it, as always, has to do with youth. This suggests that part of the answer must lie with parents and teachers and with the sort of controls (or lack of them) to which children and teenagers are subjected. Attitudes must also be important – particularly those that attach only a relative value to upholding the rule of law – as must also be policing methods (everything from swamping operations to 'no-go' areas) and race relations. However, if the question of race relations raises the whole issue of an 'under-class' in society, it is important not to accept uncritically the thesis that the answer to this problem is merely an extension of the welfare state.

The Welfare State

A Britain which in 1985 proved capable of raising so much money for famine relief in Africa can hardly, it would seem, be guilty of a lack of concern for others. Yet in the organization of its own welfare services, it is said to be facing a 'crisis of legitimacy' which has apparently been brought about by a backlash against a welfare system responsible, so it is said, for Britain's economic decline both by burdening the economy and by creating social attitudes which undermine enterprise. It has also been claimed, however, that the real crisis in welfare arises simply as a result of the cuts imposed by the recent lack of economic growth, and that the decline of the welfare state is part of the decline of Britain. Let us therefore examine these issues. Has the welfare state undermined Britain's economy? Is it now in any sense in crisis? How, once again, does Britain compare with other Western societies in this respect?

According to statistics collected by the European Commission in the 1970s, Britain appeared to be faring relatively well in the battle against poverty compared with her continental neighbours at least in so far as the incidence of relative income poverty in private households was concerned (Abel-Smith, 1983, p. 16). (See table

Table 3.8 Percentage of relative income poverty

Country	Year	% of households below poverty line (50% of disposable income)	No. of households (1,000s)
Belgium	1976	6.4	209
Denmark	1977	13.0	334
France	1975	14.8	2,630
Germany	1973	6.6	1,527
Ireland	1973	23.1	172
Italy	1978	21.8	3,823
Luxemburg	1978	14.6	16
The Netherlands	1979	4.8	233
UK	1975	6.3	1,241

Source: Abel-Smith, 1983, p. 16.

Table 3.9 Total tax revenue as percentage of GDP, 1979

Sweden	52.9
The Netherlands	47.2
Norway	46.7
Denmark	45.0
Belgium	44.5
Austria	41.2
France	41.0
West Germany	37.2
Finland	35.1
UK	33.8
Italy	33.3
Switzerland	32.8
New Zealand	31.5
USA	31.4
Canada	31.3
Portugal	25.9
Spain	25.9

Source: Abel-Smith, 1983, p. 22.

3.8.) At the same time this success does not appear to have necessitated a particularly high tax burden (table 3.9). Nor did it mean that the share of social expenditure as a percentage of GDP was relatively high either (table 3.10).

Table 3.10   Share of social expenditure as a percentage of GDP

Year	UK	USA	OECD (Europe)
1960	13.9	10.9	16.9
1965	16.2	12.3	19.7
1970	18.6	15.7	20.5
1975	22.5	20.8	27.5
1980	22.1	20.7	28.3
1981	23.7	20.8	30.0

Source: Abel-Smith, 1983, p. 22.

These figures reflect the fact that throughout the post-war period Britain has been expanding her welfare services. In housing, more homeless people are being rehoused than ever before (58,000 in 1980 compared with 33,600 in 1975) and the percentage of over-crowded households has declined from 4.89 in 1951 to 0.85 in 1976. In health care, the percentage increases in the number of hospital doctors, hospital consultants, hospital nurses, hospital mid-wives, general practitioners and health visitors/nurses between 1950 and 1980 have been 146, 218, 116, 88, 26 and 238 respectively, while life expectancy for men in the same period has increased from 66.2 years to 70.2 years and for women from 71.2 to 76.2 years. In the field of education, the schools inspectorate reported of primary schools that the results from tests were 'consistent with a rising trend in reading standards between 1955 and 1976–77' (quoted in George and Wilding, 1984, p. 50). The Bullock Report accepted that the proportion of 15-year-olds in schools who were semi-literate was 4.3 per cent in 1948 and 3.2 per cent in 1971. There are also some indications that standards of numeracy are rising. Finally, provision for the elderly and the mentally handicapped has improved. For the elderly, the number of home helps rose from 15,397 in 1953 to 46,600 in 1981, the number of home nurses from 6,829 in 1953 to 13,900 in 1979, the number of day-centre places from 11,500 in 1974 to 27,200 in 1981, while by 1981 796,000 meals were being provided by local authorities. For the mentally handicapped, the number of places in training services has rise from 10,605 in 1961 to 43,407 in 1981, while the number of places in residential hostels and homes between 1965 and 1981 has risen from 1,446 to 13,395.

Minimum standards therefore have been maintained or improved.

Inequality, however, has scarcely been eliminated. In education, for example, although substantial progress has been made in the past 20 years in the reduction of sex inequalities, inequalities of social class remain as strong as ever (something, however, that is not unique to Britain):

> Children from working-class backgrounds have a greater need of education than other children if they are to compete on more equal terms in the labour market. Yet the schools they attend are, on the whole, not as good in terms of status, teacher input and sometimes, physical surroundings. They make less use of the educational system beyond the compulsory school stage; they are less likely to pass government examinations and go on to university; and they are far more likely to end up in manual occupations, just like their fathers and mothers. (George and Wilding, 1984, p. 78)

In health care, too, despite substantial increases in expenditure, inequalities persist. Mortality rates have fallen in general but have done so more rapidly for the better-off, who make greater use of local preventive services. In housing, the provision of council housing and rate subsidies has improved amenities and reduced over-crowding for working-class tenants, yet mortgage relief was worth more to the middle classes in 1981 than subsidies were to council-house tenants (£335 on average compared to £234), while with regard to the social aspects of housing – central heating, play space, gardens, location, garages etc. – the inequalities remain.

Finally, with regard to work and earnings, 'the dispersion of gross earnings among male manual workers has changed very little during the last hundred years. The wages structure has proved extremely rigid with the lowest decile of the distribution being at around two thirds of the median wage' (George and Wilding, 1984, p. 103). It can be said that:

> manual workers not only suffer more from the costs and deprivations of the workplace than non-manual workers but they also receive lower compensation and rewards in terms of pay, fringe benefits and, in some instances, even of social security benefits. These inequalities have changed a little in some aspects as regards both the costs and rewards over the years but the striking feature is their extreme rigidity. (George and Wilding, 1984, p. 110)

Thus, if the welfare state has improved living standards over the years, it has not increased equality. Yet this should come as no surprise. First, it was not designed to increase equality but to eliminate the worst aspects of poverty; secondly, it has distracted people's attention from the whole problem of inequality by providing a single education and health system for the vast majority of the population; finally, and we shall return to this point later, its whole ethos has been one designed to support rather than to undermine the social system.

Has it encouraged or discouraged economic growth? The arguments that increased welfare provision should increase economic growth seem fairly obvious: better-educated people are more likely to perform well in a job than ill-educated ones; education reduces resistance to new ideas; by improving information and choice, increased education leads to a more rational labour market. In advanced economies further education is required to master more advanced techniques. Research, however, has drawn attention to the opposite: that more highly educated employees are not more productive; that resistance to change is influenced more by the alternative employment available; and that modern techniques have often de-skilled the production process. The real requirement for work is a solid primary education as far as the majority is concerned. Thus the link between education and economic growth is difficult to pin down. There is certainly a strong, if by no means uniform, statistical correlation between educational indicators and economic growth, but it cannot always be claimed that the relationship is one of cause and effect. Likewise, studies of the role of health care in boosting growth have also proved inconclusive. For George and Wilding:

> The general conclusion that emerges ... is that social policy has been a positive force in economic growth though not as powerful a force as some of its protagonists have claimed over the years. There is no doubt that both education and health services improve the quality of labour and in doing so they assist economic growth. Government regional and labour mobility policies have also proved their economic worth even though they have not been pursued vigorously and at the most appropriate periods. Government expenditure also encourages consumption and hence economic growth even though it may also have detrimental effects if it exceeds certain high levels ...
>
> Apart from these very specific ways, there are also the more general and non-quantifiable ways through which social policy may assist economic growth. It is quite possible that by taking care of the old, the very young, the sick and others, public services replace the old-fashioned enlarged family and make the adults more available for employment, particularly the women who were traditionally responsible for household work and bringing up children. It is also likely that by providing minimum standards of living, social services reduce public apathy and dejection and thus maintain the will to work. In a more positive way, by raising public expectations, social

76

services may for better or worse, reinforce the general belief that economic growth is and must remain the paramount objective of any government. (George and Wilding, 1984, pp. 149–50)

So much for the case for the welfare state as a proponent of economic growth. The case against it is first of all that it has channelled resources away from wealth-creating industries; secondly, that by subsidizing strikes (and indirectly trade unions) it has undermined the economy; thirdly, that it has caused high taxation which has both undermined incentives and fuelled inflation; while, finally, social security benefits are said to be so generous that they nullify the incentives to the unemployed to find work. Beyond these criticisms, there are the more general ones that welfare undermines the work ethic in general and leads to a hostility to profit-making. Is any of this true?

The first part of the criticism is based on the Bacon–Eltis thesis: the view that production in Britain fell by more than half in 1965–75 compared with the previous decade as a result of a shift in employment from manufacturing towards the public services. In short, a declining manufacturing base had to finance a growing service one, in which huge pay rises were conceded to local and central government workers. This led to economic decline: since the trade unions ensured that wages in the private sector also went up and since the extra costs could not be passed on for fear of foreign competition, the end result was decreased profit, reduced investment and less modernization of industry. The only answer to this problem was reduced public spending.

The Bacon–Eltis thesis, however, is open to a number of objections: might not the phenomena it describes be due to something else, perhaps the inefficiency of British compared with foreign industry? Why, for instance, was productivity so low in the first place? Why had industry chosen to shed labour rather than innovate or diversify? Was government policy not being blamed for defects that were already apparent? Besides, not all government expenditure is unproductive. On a less theoretical level, it was also shown that the social services did not attract redundant workers but mainly part-time female workers who were new to the labour force. And British industry was already notoriously overmanned. Moreover, with the retraction of the workforce in the public services in recent years, there has been no resurgence of jobs in manufacturing industry. Finally, it has been shown that the decline in the profitability of British industry began in the early to mid-1950s when the public sector was small and that there was no shortage of capital in the 1960s and 1970s. Hence it is difficult to see that British industry was being deprived of either labour or capital by government. As for its profits these were already being squeezed; but the real solution here would have been higher productivity, something that was never achieved.

More recently, D. R. Cameron has suggested that there is a statistically provable correlation between high levels of government spending and low capital formation. Yet his conclusion indicates that he is less than clear how it works: 'The negative coefficients between the several aspects of government spending – in particular high *levels* of spending – and the level and change in investment are not, of course, overwhelming in magnitude; moreover, they may be spurious and reflect only the existence of some unspecified factor that influences both social spending and capital formation' (Cameron, 1985, pp. 20–1). Once again, low productivity may be the answer.

The second criticism, namely that the state, through supplementary benefits, subsidizes strikes and thus undermines the economy is also one that has been overplayed. Single men on strike almost never receive any benefit; married men usually only after the first two weeks of a strike. Statistically, only a small percentage of strikers therefore receive benefit – less than 5 per cent between 1954 and 1970 and over 10 per cent only in the years of the miners' strikes. Benefits to strikers are therefore a rather meaningless factor in the argument about the economic ramifications of the welfare state.

A more important argument concerns taxation and incentives. Is it true that the welfare state leads to high taxation which discourages effort? We have already seen that compared with other countries the tax burden is not high. But more than that several opinion surveys have shown that tax is not a factor which influences work behaviour. True, people do not always behave as they say, but other surveys by econometricians seem to indicate that higher taxes, if anything, make people work harder. When all these studies were themselves weighed up by the OECD the conclusion was that: 'taxation does not have a large and significant effect in the total supply of work effort and that in particular the net effect on the labour supply of male family heads is likely to be small' (quoted in George and Wilding, 1984, p. 169). (Whether this is as true of those at the very top or the very bottom of the tax scales, however, is less clear.) Likewise, a government working group in 1967 found that it was higher salaries (pre- as well as post-tax) that led people to emigrate. Finally, the evidence also shows that high taxes do not discourage savings. These rose during the 1970s when taxes rose.

What then about the effect on work? Ever since the Poor Law Amendment Act of 1834 there has been official concern lest welfare should destroy the work ethic. Yet reviews in 1951, 1956, 1958, 1961 and 1964 by the National Assistance Board found no evidence of work-shyness. A report by the Supplementary Benefits Commission in 1978 concluded:

(a) the proportion of the unemployed who actually get more money in benefit than in work is very small. They are mainly men in the early months of unemployment for which higher benefits have been deliberately designed and when the disincentive effects seem small anyway; or men on supplementary benefit with low earnings potential and large families;

(b) this latter group are among the poorest on supplementary benefit and many of them are in poor health and have other personal problems;

(c) financial incentives cannot be considered in isolation, and in many cases may not be the major determinant of whether someone works. Of far more importance in present circumstances is whether jobs are available and offered;

(d) means-tested benefits for those in work are now of considerable significance and can make all the difference to the standard of living of low earners. Nevertheless, there is much ignorance about them and reluctance to claim them.

(quoted in George and Wilding, 1984, pp. 177–8)

Benefits fraud also turns out to be of no significance. According to statistics in 1979 (F. Field, *New Statesman*, 16 November 1979), it amounted to 0.273 per cent of all claims and to 0.027 per cent of all expenditures. Research on earnings-related benefits and family income supplements over the past decade has also failed to find any disincentive effects. Hence, the conclusion to be drawn from this review seems to be that the welfare state has played little part in Britain's economic decline and reflects instead a continuing moral concern for the poor.

What about attitudes? Does social welfare lead to socialism? Is there any evidence that the mere existence of a welfare state serves to undermine an otherwise healthy faith in private competition? George and Wilding assert the very opposite. Far from undermining capitalism, the social services play a crucial part in maintaining the capitalist system: 'whatever their critics may say and think, social services do ease problems which could prove socially and politically disruptive. Discontents are allayed, potential critics are mollified, the legitimacy of government and the existing political order is enhanced. Political debate centres on the middle ground and challenges to the political consensus are easily dismissed. Stability is therefore enhanced' (George and Wilding, 1984, p. 194).

The social services, it is argued, do this in a number of ways: adopting non-challenging views of social problems; tackling individual 'cases' not systemic problems. Misfortune is always classified as individual – so too is the remedy – with the result that the 'system' is absolved from blame. These services are also accused of encouraging and rewarding certain values while punishing others: stigmatizing economic failure, encouraging thrift and work, shaming those who actually claim their benefits. The impression is fostered that private provision must inevitably be superior, while schools socialize their pupils to be hard-working, conforming and successful. Schools also accustom pupils to systems of hierarchy and authority and integrate their pupils into the economic system. Finally, it is alleged that social services contribute to the replacement of class conflict by group conflict. This is less threatening to authority and thus leaves it more secure: the challenge to the government is weaker when its opponents are split between claimants and non-claimants, tenants and owner-occupiers, private and state pupils, and when nurses, teachers, academics and social workers have to compete with one another for the same resources.

Much of this can be confirmed from a non-Marxist viewpoint. Peter Taylor-Gooby's (1985) latest review of opinion-surveys indicates increasing support not merely for the welfare state (and increased taxation if necessary to support it) but also for capitalism. It also shows that support for certain claims – child allowance and unemployment benefit – is markedly less strong than support for education, pensions and the health service. Finally, the better-off believe that the poorest benefit most, while the latter are of the opinion that it is the better-off who do so.

It would seem, therefore, that Professor Dahrendorf might well be correct in assuming that the welfare state must have a role to play in maintaining social harmony. That, apparently, has been one of its most vital functions until now and the clear wish of the vast majority is that it should be maintained in the future. Yet Dahrendorf believes that the welfare state is in a crisis primarily because of lack of economic growth and economic resources. Others (King, 1975; Brittan, 1975) have spoken of a 'legitimation crisis' due to 'overload' – too many administrative demands being imposed on the state in the field of welfare; or too many expectations arising from its success in the past. Under Mrs Thatcher, it must be admitted, an attempt has been made to reduce the role of the state. Yet public spending has increased, benefits have mostly retained their value and the welfare state has been preserved. The latest research even suggests that there will be room for expansion in the future.

> When the consequent public expenditure aggregates are examined, it is clear that provided economic growth is of the order of 1 per cent or more annually, there is no public expenditure crisis. At these levels of economic growth a restrictive budgetary stance, which nonetheless maintained the general standards of public services, ought to see programme expenditure growing at about the rate of GDP. At higher rates of economic growth (which seem more likely) a relaxation in the degree of budgetary restrictiveness is still compatible with a decline in programme expenditure relative to GDP. Unless the govern-

ment seeks absolute cuts in the level of public expenditure, very sharp cuts in its relative share of GDP or is concerned that public revenues will or should grow more slowly than GDP, these data do not suggest any need for more radical policies to cut public spending.

Interpreted from a different perspective, the data suggest that within the likely range of economic growth levels there is scope for matching changes in social need and indeed for some increase in the real level of social policy expenditure, without increasing the overall share of programme expenditure within GDP. Obviously if the latter share is increased the scope of improvement is correspondingly greater. (O'Higgins and Patterson, 1985, p. 129)

The welfare state, therefore, seems destined to be a constant in British political and social life rather than a variable. It has most likely already reached its apex but no evidence suggests that Britain's political system could easily survive without it.

4 Conclusion

Before the 1960s British self-confidence had been boosted by victory in two world wars, the successful transformation of Empire into Commonwealth, a world role in international affairs and a consciousness of parliamentary government and the rule of law going back over centuries. As a result there was great confidence in British institutions. Indeed, the British system of government, 'the Westminster model', was held up to developed and underdeveloped nations alike as a paradigm of democratic rule. Since the 1960s, however, most British political institutions – the monarchy excepted – have experienced public criticism. The result is that the 'Westminster model' is no longer displayed to all and sundry as an object of automatic emulation and has itself been modified. Indeed, the range of modification has been considerable: the introduction of the referendum on major matters of debate (continuing membership of the Common Market, the retention of Ulster within the United Kingdom, proposed devolution for Scotland and Wales); the establishment of Select Committees in the House of Commons; the surrender of parliamentary sovereignty to the EEC; the abolition of the Stormont Parliament in Northern Ireland; the introduction of paid political advisers for Ministers; the creation and abolition of the so-called 'Think Tank'; the reform of the Civil Service. Indeed, if the devolution proposals, as well as others introduced to reform the House of Lords, had been passed into law, one would today be writing not of the modification but of the total transformation of British government since the 1970s.

All this is significant because it surely proves that the 'British disease', whatever else it may be, is not one of failure to respond to public pressure for institutional change. Indeed, further change may well be on the way: there is already considerable pressure to alter the constitutional role of judges by enacting a Bill of Rights; likewise there is much pressure to reform the voting system. The party system has also seen much change. Whereas in 1950 about 98 per cent of voters opted either for the Conservative or Labour party, today the figure is only about 70 per cent, given the rise of the SDP–Liberal Alliance (not to mention the Scottish and Welsh Nationalists). It would seem safe to conclude, therefore, that Britain has responded politically and institutionally to pressure for change without in any sense indulging in extremism. This is not usually the experience of a country in decline.

Indeed, from all the historical trends which have been examined in this book, it would appear that the case supporting Britain's decline can be sustained on one level only. True, there have been urban riots and there has been a worrying increase in crime statistics, but it is probably the case that people are relatively safer nowadays than in times past. The statistics, as we have seen, are open to a variety of interpretations.

The case for a moral decline is almost impossible to sustain. British values remain stubbornly traditional; marriage is more popular than ever; and the concessions which have been made to different life-styles have been relatively limited. Indeed, it is the intensely conservative nature of British society which makes the changes appear so radical to their opponents. Other Western European and North American societies have gone much further in enacting social reform.

Be that as it may, Britain has become a more tolerant society since the war. It is also one which, to its credit, still demands state action on behalf of the less fortunate members of society, gives generously to charities of all sorts and which still enjoys a stable and politically sensitive democracy. Even its economy is growing again and levels of production and standards of living are at an all-time high, albeit for those in work. The long-term problem of relative economic decline has not yet been solved, but at least it forms the centre of the political debate and is being tackled vigorously, if controversially. It is far too early yet to tell what success, if any, will be accorded to these efforts but the level of the debate can only be lifted if citizens bring to it a proper awareness of the arguments.

References

Abel-Smith, Brian, 1983: 'Assessing the balance sheet', in Glennester, H. (ed.) *The Future of the Welfare State*. London.

Abrams, M., Gerard, D. and Timms, N. (eds) 1985: *Values and Social Change in Britain*. Basingstoke.

Alford, B. W. E. 1981: 'New industries for old? British industry between the wars', in Floud, R. and McCloskey, D. (eds) *The Economic History of Britain since 1700*, vol 2: *1860 to the 1970s*. Cambridge.

Alter, Peter 1978: 'Staat und Wissenschaft in Grossbritannien vor 1914', in Berding, H. et al. (eds) *Vom Staat des Ancien Regime zum Modernen Parteistaat*. Oldenburg.

Bacon, R. and Eltis, W. 1976: *Britain's Economic Problem: Too Few Producers*. London.

Barnett, Correlli 1986. *Audit of War*. London.

Bell, Josephine 1962: *Crime in our Time*. London.

Boswell, John 1980: *Christianity, Social Tolerance and Homosexuality: Gay People in Western Europe from the Beginning of the Christian Era to the Fourteenth Century*. Chicago.

Brittan, S. 1975: 'The economic contradictions of democracy', *British Journal of Political Science*, vol. 5, no. 1.

Buxton, N. K. 1979: 'Introduction', in Buxton, N. K. and Aldcroft, D. H. (eds) *British Industry between the Wars: Instability and Industrial Development, 1919–1939*. London.

Cairncross, Alex 1981: 'The post-war years', in Floud, R. and McCloskey, D. (eds) *The Economic History of Britain since 1700*, vol. 2: *1860 to the 1970s*. Cambridge.

Cameron, D. R. 1985: 'Public expenditure and economic performance in international perspective', in Klein, R. and O'Higgins, M. (eds) *The Future of Welfare*. London.

Chalmers, Malcolm 1985: *Paying for Defence: Military Spending and British Decline*. London.

Coleman, D. C. 1969: *Courtaulds: an Economic and Social History, II: Rayon*. Oxford.

Dahrendorf, Ralf 1985: *Law and Order* (The Hamlyn Lectures for 1985). London.

Davies, Christie 1975: *Permissive Britain: Social Change in the Sixties and Seventies*. London.

Drummond, I. 1981: 'Britain and the world economy', in Floud, R. and McClockey, D. (eds) *The Economic History of Britain since 1700*, vol. 2: *1860 to the 1970s*. Cambridge.

Fischer, Wolfram 1983: *Germany in the World Economy during the Nineteenth Century*, The Annual Lecture, The German Historical Institute, London.

Fraser, W. Hamish 1981: *The Coming of the Mass Market, 1850–1914*. London.

Gamble, Andrew 1981: *Britain in Decline*. London.

George, V. and Wilding, P. 1984: *The Impact of Social Policy*. London.

Gillis, John 1986: *For Better or Worse: British Marriages 1600 to the Present*. Oxford.

Glennester, Howard (ed.) 1983: *The Future of the Welfare State: Remaking Social Policy*. London.

Gomulka, Stanislaw 1978: 'Britain's slow industrial growth: increasing inefficiency versus low rate of technological change', in Beckerman, W. (ed.) *Slow Growth in Britain: Cause and Consequences*. Oxford.

Hannah, C. 1974: 'Managerial innovation and the rise of the large-scale company in inter-war Britain', *Economic History Review*, 2nd series, vol. 27.

Harris, Jose and Thane, Pat 1984: 'British and European bankers, 1880–1914', in Thane, P., Crossick, G. and Floud, R. (eds) *The Power of the Past (Essays for Eric Hobsbawm)*. Cambridge.

Hinton, Thomas R. 1973: 'German and English intellectuals: contrasts and comparisons', in Feuchtwanger, E. J. (ed.) *Upheaval and Continuity: a Century of German History*. London.

Hofstadter, Richard 1955: *The Age of Reform*. New York.

Hofstadter, Richard 1966: *Anti-intellectualism in American Life*. New York.

Howard League Working Party Report 1985: *Unlawful Sex, Offences, Victims and Offenders in the Criminal Justice System of England and Wales*. London.

Karlinsky, Simon 1984: 'Decadence', in Denney, M., Ortleb, C. and Steele, T. (eds) *The View from Christopher Street*. London.

King, A. 1975: 'Overload: problems of governing in the 1970s', *Political Studies*, vol. 23, nos 1 and 2.

Kinsey, A., Pomeroy, W. and Martin, C. 1948: *Sexual Behaviour in the Human Male*. Philadelphia.

Kinsey, A., Pomeroy, W. and Martin, C. 1953: *Sexual Behaviour in the Human Female*. Philadelphia.

Kirby, M. W. 1981: *The Decline of British Economic Power since 1870*. London.

Manser, W. A. P. 1971: *Britain in Balance: the myth of failure*. Harmondsworth.

Mount, F. 1982: *The Subversive Family, An Alternative History of Love and Marriage*. London.

Norman, E. R. 1976: *Church and Society in England 1770–1970: a Historical Study*. Oxford.

Nossiter, Bernard 1978: *Britain: a Future that Works*. London.

O'Higgins, M. and Patterson, A. 1985: 'The prospects for public expenditure: a disaggregate analysis', in Klein, R. and O'Higgins, M. (eds) *The Future of Welfare*. London.

Pollard, S. 1982: *The Wasting of the British Economy*. London.

Read, D. 1979: *England, 1868–1914*. London.

Richardson, H. W. 1962: 'The basis of economic recovery in the 1930s: a review and a new interpretation', *Economic History Review*, 2nd series, vol. 15.

Rubenstein, W. D. 1974: 'British millionaires, 1809–1949', *Bulletin of the Institute of Historical Research*, vol. 48.

Rubenstein, W. D. 1981: 'New men of wealth and the purchase of land in nineteenth century Britain', *Past and Present*, vol. 92.

Sandberg, L. G. 1981: 'The entrepreneur and technological change', in Floud, R. and McCloskey, D. (eds) *The Economic History of Britain since 1700*, vol. 2: *1860 to the 1970s*. Cambridge.

Saul, S. B. 1979: *Industrialisation and De-industrialisation? The Interaction of the German and British Economies before the First World War*, The Annual Lecture, The German Historical Institute, London.

Smith, Keith 1984: *The British Economic Crisis*. London.

Stern, Fritz 1965: *The Politics of Cultural Despair. A Study in the Rise of the German Ideology*. New York.

Taylor-Gooby, P. 1985: 'The politics of welfare: public attitudes and behaviour', in Klein, R. and O'Higgins, M. (eds) *The Future of Welfare*. London.

Thomas, T. 1981: 'Aggregate demand in the United Kingdom, 1918–45', in Floud, R. and McCloskey, D. (eds) *The Economic History of Britain since 1700*, vol. 2: *1860 to the 1970s*. Cambridge.

Thompson, F. M. L. 1984: 'English landed society in the nineteenth century', in Thane, P., Crossick, G. and Floud, R. (eds) *The Power of the Past (Essays for Eric Hobsbawm)*. Cambridge.

Tracey, M. and Morrison, D. 1979: *Whitehouse*. London.

Turner, H. A. 1969: *Is Britain Really Strike Prone?: a review of the incidence, character and costs of industrial conflict*. Cambridge.

Walker, Nigel 1965: *Crime and Punishment in Britain: an analysis of the penal system in theory, law and practice*. Edinburgh.

Warwick, Paul 1985: 'Did Britain change? An inquiry into the causes of national decline', *Journal of Contemporary History*, vol. 20, no. 1.

Weeks, Jeffrey 1981: *Sex, Politics and Society: the Regulation of Sexuality since 1800*. London.

Wiener, Martin J. 1981: *English Culture and the Decline of the Industrial Spirit, 1850–1980*. Cambridge.

Index

technology, British, new: 1870–1914
     12, 13–15, 20
  1914–39   22
  1939 to present 36
Thatcher, Margaret 11, 41, 80
Thatcherism 39
Theatres Act 1968 46–7
'third generation decline' 13–14
Third World, industrialization in 23
Thomas, T. 22
Thompson, F. M. L. 8–9
tolerance 69, 83
  and military values 53
  and permissiveness 56
tourism, as growth area 4
Tracey, M. and Morrison, D. 41–2,
     44, 54
trade unions, as constraint on growth
     11, 37–8, 77
Tucholsky, K. 7
Turner, H. A. 37

'under-class', concept of 71–2
unemployment: 1870–1914 16
  after First World War 21–2, 26
  after Second World War 29, 38
urbanization, growth of 16, 49
USA: crime rates 57, 72
  defence expenditure 34
  effects of First World War 21, 22–3
  growth in exports 13
  imperialism 5
  industrial spirit 6, 14, 18

investment levels 36
labour force 15
productivity 21, 26
sexual revolution 52
trade with Britain 19–20
urbanization 16

Values Survey, see Abrams, M. et al.
violence: increase in 41, 57–8, 65–6,
     69, 71–2
  on television and film 48, 54

wage rates: 1870–1914 14–15
  post Second World War 3, 75, 77
Walker, Nigel 60, 61–2, 64–6, 68
Warwick, Paul 5–6
Weeks, Jeffrey 47–8, 50, 60–1
welfare state 40, 70–2
  and economic decline 72, 76–81
  legitimation crisis 72, 80
  standards of provision 73–6, 83
  see also intervention, government
Whitehouse, Mary 40, 41, 42–3, 54
Wiener, Martin 6–7, 9
Wolfenden Committee Report 1957
     60–1
women, status of 46, 50, 56, 57, 76
work ethic 8, 53, 72, 77, 78–9
world economy 19–20, 22–3

youth, and crime levels 65–8, 72
'youth revolution' 50

Index by Meg Davies